THE TRAVELLER

AND

THE DESERTED VILLAGE

GOLDSMITH

THE TRAVELLER

AND

THE DESERTED VILLAGE

EDITED BY

W. MURISON, M.A.

CAMBRIDGE
AT THE UNIVERSITY PRESS
1936

CAMBRIDGE
UNIVERSITY PRESS

University Printing House, Cambridge CB2 8BS, United Kingdom

Published in the United States of America by Cambridge University Press, New York

Cambridge University Press is part of the University of Cambridge.

It furthers the University's mission by disseminating knowledge in the pursuit of education, learning and research at the highest international levels of excellence.

www.cambridge.org
Information on this title: www.cambridge.org/9781107682610

© Cambridge University Press 1906

First edition 1906
First published 1906
Reprinted 1922, 1934, 1936
First paperback edition 2014

A catalogue record for this publication is available from the British Library

ISBN 978-1-107-68261-0 Paperback

NOTE.

THE Editor has read these poems several times with classes of boys; and the most of the material, both in the Introduction and in the Notes, has been tested in class-teaching.

CONTENTS.

INTRODUCTION.

I. LIFE OF GOLDSMITH[1].

OLIVER GOLDSMITH was born at Pallas in County Longford, November 10, 1728. His father, a clergyman of the Church of Ireland, came of a family originally English but long settled in Ireland. In 1730 the Rev. Charles Goldsmith succeeded to the living of Kilkenny West, and with his family removed to Lissoy in County Westmeath, a few miles from Pallas. After Oliver had been taught his letters by Elizabeth Delap, who called him "impenetrably stupid," he was sent at the age of six to Lissoy school, then in the charge of Thomas Byrne, a veteran quartermaster of the Spanish Wars in the beginning of the century. Oliver continued slow at lessons : he was fonder of reading chap books, listening to ballads, and trying to make rhymes. About this time he suffered from small-pox, which disfigured him for life. After attending several schools, he went as sizar to Trinity College, Dublin, where his life was far from smooth. A rough tutor harassed Oliver, who preferred idling and frolic to study. More than once he came into collision with the University authorities. When he graduated B.A. in 1749, he was lowest on the list. He had been noted for his skill in

[1] For fuller information consult the following : article in *Dictionary of National Biography*; Forster's *Life and Adventures of Oliver Goldsmith*, Seventh Edition, 2 vols., 1877 ; Black's *Goldsmith* (English Men of Letters) ; Austin Dobson's *Goldsmith* (Great Writers) ; Macaulay's article in *Encyclopaedia Britannica*, which is also in his *Miscellaneous Writings*; and Austin Dobson's article in *Chambers's Encyclopaedia.*

turning Horace's odes : he would often write ballads at five shillings each, and had great delight in hearing them sung and applauded in Dublin streets.

For a year or two after graduation, he lived chiefly in his mother's house at Ballymahon : his father had died in 1747. His brother Henry, now rector of the parish, sometimes got his assistance in teaching ; but, as a rule, Oliver haunted the Ballymahon inn, told stories, played the flute, took solitary walks on summer evenings along the river, and shared in the sports on the village green : in hammer throwing he once won the prize at Ballymahon Fair. He was refused orders by the Bishop : tradition says it was because he appeared for ordination in "scarlet breeches." Then he started for America, but never got further than Cork. He was the despair of his relatives, but an uncle, Contarine by name, furnished him with £50 to enable him to study law in London. The money, however, was won by Dublin gamblers, and Oliver went home in shame. His uncle equipped him again, this time to go to Edinburgh ; and Oliver left Ireland, never to return.

He reached Edinburgh in 1752, and after a stay of nearly two years set off to Leyden to continue his studies. From here he started early in 1755 to make "the grand tour" of Europe on foot. At Louvain he may have got the degree of M.B.—or it may have been at Padua. He wandered on through France, Germany, Switzerland, Italy, Carinthia, and back through France to England. The details of his journeying are quite uncertain. Food and shelter he said he obtained by playing the flute or by disputing at the universities.

Landing penniless at Dover in February, 1756, he came to London, where he was in turn apothecary's assistant, physician, proof-reader and usher. Then he wrote for the bookseller Griffiths. In 1759 he published *An Enquiry into the Present State of Polite Learning*, which gained him fame, and the friendship of several literary men. He also started a periodical, *The Bee*. Next year to the *Public Ledger* he contributed the *Chinese Letters*, afterwards published with the title *The Citizen*

of the World. Their brilliant sketches of character still further
raised his literary reputation. In 1764 he was one of the nine
original members of the Club variously known as "The Literary
Club," or "Dr Johnson's Club." Johnson once remarked to
Boswell, "Dr Goldsmith is one of the first men we now have
as an author, and he is a very worthy man too." In December,
1764, *The Traveller* was published, and its author was hailed as
in the front rank of living poets. "I shall never more think
Mr Goldsmith ugly," said the sister of Sir Joshua Reynolds on
hearing the poem read. Two years later *The Vicar of Wakefield*
marked Goldsmith as among the foremost novelists. His
comedy, *The Good-natured Man,* was produced in 1768. All this
time he had been busy with histories and other hack-work for
the booksellers. His next poem, *The Deserted Village,* published in 1770, was instantly popular. Another comedy, *She
Stoops to Conquer,* 1773, was very successful. Next year in
April, Goldsmith died, and was buried in the burying-ground
of the Temple Church. Soon after his death appeared his
Retaliation and his *History of the Earth and Animated Nature.*
In 1776 a monument was erected in Westminster Abbey with
Dr Johnson's Latin epitaph.

As a writer Goldsmith is remarkable for his versatility: the
most diverse kinds of literature he tried with unvarying success.
His works show wide knowledge of men, kindly humour and
sympathy, inimitable clearness, beauty and grace of style.
With perfect truth Dr Johnson's epitaph states that Goldsmith
had tried every variety of literature, and none that he touched
did he fail to adorn—"nullum quod tetigit non ornavit." In
sharp contrast with his deftness as a writer, he often showed a
blundering hesitation in conversation. This was hit off with
cleverness but exaggeration in the epitaph which Garrick com-
posed in sport:

> "Here lies Nolly Goldsmith for shortness called Noll,
> Who wrote like an angel, but talked like poor Poll."

At the time Goldsmith had no reply ready, but began to

elaborate one, *Retaliation*, unfinished at his death. In it are striking sketches of Burke, Garrick, and Reynolds. Goldsmith, however, did not always fail in conversation. Once when relating the fable of the little fishes who petitioned Jupiter, he saw Dr Johnson laughing at him, and said: "Why, Dr Johnson, this is not so easy as you seem to think; for if you were to make little fishes talk, they would talk like WHALES."

Goldsmith's nature was sensitive, and he keenly felt neglect and hostile criticism. He had a touch of vanity, which appeared in his love of gay clothes. He was lavish in expenditure, yet that was often the effect of his overflowing kindness of heart, for, like his Village Preacher,

"His pity gave ere charity began."

"But," said Dr Johnson, "let not his frailties be remembered: he was a very great man." And we may add this. One who was the friend of Dr Johnson, of Sir Joshua Reynolds, and of Edmund Burke, could have been no mean man.

II. *THE TRAVELLER* AND *THE DESERTED VILLAGE.*

Though *The Traveller* was not published till December, 1764, part of it, as Goldsmith tells us in the dedication, had been written nearly ten years before and sent home to his brother Henry. It is a didactic poem, the purpose of which is thus declared: "I have endeavoured to show, that there may be equal happiness in states, that are differently governed from our own; that every state has a particular principle of happiness; and that this principle in each may be carried to a mischievous excess[1]." Macaulay summarizes the poem as follows: "An English wanderer, seated on a crag among the Alps, near the point where three great countries meet, looks

[1] See p. 4. Compare these passages in *The Traveller*, lines 75 sqq., 93 sqq., 429 sqq.

down on the boundless prospect, reviews his long pilgrimage, recalls the varieties of scenery, of climate, of government, of religion, of national character, which he has observed, and comes to the conclusion, just or unjust, that our happiness depends little on political institutions, and much on the temper and regulation of our own minds[1]." It is true that, even under the best form of government, there must be much unhappiness; but it is certain that a bad form of government, or any form badly administered, is the direct cause of much misery. Goldsmith's teaching then is open to objection, but we are not so much concerned with the teaching. The poetry is what is most important for us; and that is at its best, not in the moralizing passages, but in those which illustrate the theme, particularly where Goldsmith gives personal experiences and reminiscences, as in the passage beginning:

" Gay, sprightly land of mirth and social ease "

(241 sqq.).

The time favoured the appearance of the poem. Very little poetry had been published for several years; and Dr Johnson's criticism was well deserved—" a production to which, since the death of Pope, it would not be easy to find anything equal." His words to Boswell were even more emphatic: "There has not been so fine a poem since Pope's time."

The theme of *The Deserted Village* had been outlined in *The Traveller*:

" Have we not seen, round Britain's peopled shore,
Her useful sons exchanged for useless ore?
*   *   *   *   *   *
Have we not seen, at pleasure's lordly call,
The smiling long-frequented village fall?
Beheld the duteous son, the sire decayed,
The modest matron, and the blushing maid,
Forced from their homes, a melancholy train,
To traverse climes beyond the western main?"

(397 sqq.).

[1] *Encyclopaedia Britannica*, art. "Goldsmith."

In *The Deserted Village*, a son of the village, who remembers it in its prosperous days, and who, amid all his many wanderings, hoped to return home at last, is represented as coming back only to find sweet Auburn deserted and in ruins. He recalls the simple merry rustic life, the clergyman, the school-master, the village inn. He pictures the villagers suffering the woes of exile in an unkindly land ; and he curses trade as causing the luxury that produced this depopulation. The population of England was indeed shifting at this time, but it was increasing. The economic aspect of the poem, however, does not concern us. Nor yet does the precise locality of Auburn matter much. Some maintain that it is in England, others in Ireland. According to Macaulay, the picture in the poem "is made up of incongruous parts. The village in its happy days is a true English village. The village in its decay is an Irish village[1]." This incongruity, if incongruity it be, was just reversed in Goldsmith's own mind. He distinctly says that he saw the depopulation in England and maintains this in spite of contradiction. "I know you will object (and indeed several of our best and wisest friends concur in the opinion) that the depopulation it deplores is nowhere to be seen....To this I can scarcely make any other answer than that I sincerely believe what I have written; that I have taken all possible pains, in my country excursions, for these four or five years past, to be certain of what I allege[2]." Now, from 1765 to 1770 the only country Goldsmith was in, was England. Again, the village in its prosperity was in Ireland : it was Lissoy, seen through the medium of years of exile, and naturally appearing in a rosy light. But it is not the topography of the poem that is important : it is the melody of the verse, the simplicity, the natural scene-painting, the sympathy with suffering men and women.

[1] *Encyclopaedia Britannica*, art. "Goldsmith."
[2] See p. 23.

III. GOLDSMITH'S VERSE.

The metre of the two poems is the Heroic Couplet. Heroic verse—so called because much used for heroic subjects—is the iambic pentameter, that is, lines of five iambic feet. Iambic, of course, means in English an unaccented syllable followed by an accented, not a short and a long syllable as in Greek or Latin. Heroic verse may be either unrhymed—blank verse— or rhymed. Here we have the lines rhyming in pairs, a very favourite metre in English since Chaucer's time. In the 18th century Pope elaborated the Heroic Couplet, and had many followers. Goldsmith condemned[1] the use of blank verse and of irregular measures; and in practice he sought to follow the traditional metre. But, as he stood midway between the "town" poets of Queen Anne and the early Georges, and the nature poets of the 19th century, so his couplet, though formally the same as Pope's or Johnson's, differs widely in melody, in grace, in freedom from monotony. Read aloud, for example, and compare with a passage from Pope, either the lines in *The Traveller* beginning

" To kinder skies, where gentler manners reign "

(239 sqq.),

or those in *The Deserted Village* beginning

" Sweet was the sound, when oft at evening's close "

(113 sqq.).

These passages also show that, unlike Pope, Goldsmith built up his verse in paragraphs, not in couplets.

In rhyming, Goldsmith is singularly correct. On this point we must remember that the pronunciation of words is constantly changing, and consequently what seems to us a faulty rhyme now, may have been a good rhyme formerly.

[1] See p. 4.

Pope's *Rape of the Lock*, III. 7-8, supplies an example of this:

> "Here thou, great Anna! whom three realms obey,
> Dost sometimes counsel take—and sometimes tea."

Allowing, however, for change of pronunciation, we find that Goldsmith possessed a far finer ear for rhyme than, for instance, Pope and Keats. The latter's poems bristle with defective rhymes—'smoke, took,' 'long, sung,' 'rose, lose,' 'higher, Thalia,' 'rushes, bushes,' 'was, pass,' 'thorns, fawns.' These two poems of Goldsmith contain only a dozen faulty rhymes, more than half of which are those permitted in English by convention, the so-called eye-rhymes. An eye-rhyme occurs in *The Deserted Village*, 29-30, where 'love' is rhymed with 'reprove.' In the same poem other defective rhymes are 79-80, 187-8, 205-6, 231-2, 361-2; and in *The Traveller*, 3-4, 21-2, 79-80, 151-2, 243-4, 379-80.

Goldsmith is also conspicuously free from the artificial diction of the 18th century. It is true he writes,

> "No cheerful murmurs fluctuate in the gale"
> (*The Deserted Village*, 126),

a line which Matthew Arnold brands as "rhetorical, ornate— and, poetically, quite false." It is true he calls foaming ale "mantling bliss" (*The Deserted Village*, 248). But natural language is far more common; as,

> "The noisy geese that gabbled o'er the pool"
> (*The Deserted Village*, 119);

or,

> "Sweet as the primrose peeps beneath the thorn"
> (*The Deserted Village*, 330).

In simplicity of diction Goldsmith compares favourably with Pope, Thomson and Cowper. Sheep are in Pope "fleecy care" (*Messiah*, 49), and in Thomson "soft fearful people" (*Summer*, 378). Barndoor fowls are in Thomson "the household feathery people" (*Winter*, 87), and in Cowper "the feathered tribes domestic" (*The Task*, V. 62). Cowper calls tea "the fragrant lymph" (*The Task*, III. 391), and the sap of trees "the pure and subtle lymph" (*The Task*, VI. 135).

CHRONOLOGICAL TABLE.

Goldsmith's Life.		*Contemporary Events.*
1747	His father dies.	1747 Gray's *Eton College Ode.*
		1748 Thomson's *Castle of Indolence.* Richardson's *Clarissa Harlowe.* Thomson dies.
1749	Graduates. Goes to Bally-mahon.	1749 Fielding's *Tom Jones.* Johnson's *Vanity of Human Wishes.* The *Monthly Review* begins.
		1750 Johnson begins *The Rambler.*
		1751 Gray's *Elegy.* New style of dating introduced.
1752	To Edinburgh to study medicine.	1752 Fanny Burney born.
1754	At Leyden.	1754 Crabbe born. Fielding dies.
1755	Walking through various countries of Europe. Part of *The Traveller* written.	1755 First Edition of Johnson's *Dictionary.* Braddock defeated at Fort Duquesne. (See Thackeray's *Virginians.*)
1756–58	Returns to England and tries various occupations.	
		1757 Gray's *Pindaric Odes.* Battle of Plassey.
		1758 Johnson begins *The Idler.* The British capture Fort Duquesne, and thus secure the Ohio region.
1759	*An Enquiry into the Present State of Polite Learning in Europe.*	1759 Johnson's *Rasselas.* Sterne's *Tristram Shandy*, vols. I. and II. Burns born. British Museum opened. Capture of Quebec.
1760	*Chinese Letters* begin.	1760 George III.'s accession.
		1761 Richardson dies.

Goldsmith's Life.

Contemporary Events.

1762 *Citizen of the World (Chinese Letters).*

1762 Macpherson's *Ossian.* Bute becomes Prime Minister. Dr Johnson accepts pension.

1763 Churchill's *Prophecy of Famine.* Wilkes prosecuted for No. 45 of *North Briton*: riots in his favour. Johnson meets Boswell.

1764 "The Club": among the original members—Dr Johnson, Reynolds, Burke, Goldsmith. Other early members—Garrick, Gibbon, Adam Smith. *The Traveller.*

1764 Churchill dies.

1765 Percy's *Reliques.* Stamp Act.

1766 *Vicar of Wakefield.*

1768 *The Good-natured Man.* Henry Goldsmith dies.

1768 Sterne dies. Riots in favour of Wilkes.

1769 Burke's *Observations on the Present State of the Nation.* First letter of "Junius."

1770 *The Deserted Village.*

1770 Burke's *Thoughts on the Present Discontents.* Whigs broken up. North becomes Prime Minister. Wordsworth born.

1771 Gray dies. Scott born. The Commons seek in vain to stop publication of debates.

1772 Coleridge born.

1773 *She Stoops to Conquer.*

1773 Boston "Tea Party."

Goldsmith's Life.   *Contemporary Events.*

1774 Goldsmith dies. *Retalia-*   1774 Burke's *Speech on American*
      tion. A History of the   *Taxation.* Southey born.
      Earth and Animated   Warren Hastings, Gover-
      Nature.   nor General of India.

                                      1775 Burke's *Speech on Concilia-*
                                            tion with America. John-
                                            son's *Journey to the*
                                            Western Islands. Lamb
                                            born. War with Ameri-
                                            can Colonists.

1776 Monument in Westminster   1776 Gibbon's *Decline and Fall*
      Abbey erected to Gold-   *of the Roman Empire,*
      smith : "qui nullum fere   vol. I. Adam Smith's
      scribendi genus non teti-   *Wealth of Nations.* De-
      git, nullum quod tetigit   claration of Indepen-
      non ornavit."   dence.

THE TRAVELLER

OR

A PROSPECT OF SOCIETY

DEDICATION.

To the Rev. Henry Goldsmith.

Dear Sir,

  I am sensible that the friendship between us can acquire no new force from the ceremonies of a Dedication; and perhaps it demands an excuse thus to prefix your name to my attempts, which you decline giving with your own. 5 *But as a part of this Poem was formerly written to you from Switzerland, the whole can now, with propriety, be only inscribed to you. It will also throw a light upon many parts of it, when the reader understands that it is addressed to a man who, despising fame and fortune, has retired early* 10 *to happiness and obscurity, with an income of forty pounds a year.*

  I now perceive, my dear brother, the wisdom of your humble choice. You have entered upon a sacred office, where the harvest is great and the labourers are but few; while 15 *you have left the field of ambition, where the labourers are many and the harvest not worth carrying away. But of all kinds of ambition, what from the refinement of the times, from different systems of criticism, and from the divisions of party, that which pursues poetical fame is the wildest.* 20

  Poetry makes a principal amusement among unpolished nations; but in a country verging to the extremes of refinement, Painting and Music come in for a share. As these offer the feeble mind a less laborious entertainment, they at first rival Poetry and at length supplant her; they engross 25 *all that favour once shown to her, and though but younger sisters, seize upon the elder's birthright.*

  Yet, however this art may be neglected by the powerful,

1 — 2

it is *still in greater danger from the mistaken efforts of the*
30 *learned to improve it. What criticisms have we not heard*
of late in favour of blank verse, and Pindaric odes, choruses,
anapests and iambics, alliterative care and happy negligence!
Every absurdity has now a champion to defend it; and as he
is generally much in the wrong, so he has always much to
35 *say; for error is ever talkative.*

But there is an *enemy to this art still more dangerous—*
I mean party. Party entirely distorts the judgment, and
destroys the taste. When the mind is once infected with this
disease, it can only find pleasure in what contributes to
40 *increase the distemper. Like the tiger, that seldom desists*
from pursuing man after having once preyed upon human
flesh, the reader who has once gratified his appetite with
calumny, makes ever after the most agreeable feast upon
murdered reputation. Such readers generally admire some
45 *half-witted thing, who wants to be thought a bold man,*
having lost the character of a wise one. Him they dignify
with the name of poet; his tawdry lampoons are called
satires; his turbulence is said to be force, and his frenzy
fire.

50 *What reception a poem may find, which has neither abuse,*
party, nor blank verse to support it, I cannot tell, nor am
I solicitous to know. My aims are right. Without espousing
the cause of any party, I have attempted to moderate the rage
of all. I have endeavoured to show that there may be equal
55 *happiness in states that are differently governed from our own;*
that every state has a particular principle of happiness; and
this principle in each may be carried to a mischievous excess.
There are few can judge better than yourself how far these
positions are illustrated in this poem.

60 *I am, Dear Sir,*
Your most affectionate Brother,
OLIVER GOLDSMITH.

THE TRAVELLER;

OR,

A PROSPECT OF SOCIETY.

Remote, unfriended, melancholy, slow,
Or by the lazy Scheldt, or wandering Po;
Or onward, where the rude Carinthian boor
Against the houseless stranger shuts the door;
Or where Campania's plain forsaken lies,   5
A weary waste expanding to the skies;
Where'er I roam, whatever realms to see,
My heart untravelled fondly turns to thee;
Still to my brother turns, with ceaseless pain,
And drags at each remove a lengthening chain. 10

 Eternal blessings crown my earliest friend,
And round his dwelling guardian saints attend:
Blest be that spot, where cheerful guests retire
To pause from toil, and trim their evening fire:
Blest that abode, where want and pain repair, 15
And every stranger finds a ready chair:
Blest be those feasts with simple plenty crowned,
Where all the ruddy family around
Laugh at the jests or pranks that never fail,
Or sigh with pity at some mournful tale;   20

Or press the bashful stranger to his food,
And learn the luxury of doing good.

But me, not destined such delights to share,
My prime of life in wandering spent and care,
Impelled, with steps unceasing, to pursue   25
Some fleeting good, that mocks me with the view;
That, like the circle bounding earth and skies,
Allures from far, yet, as I follow, flies;
My fortune leads to traverse realms alone,
And find no spot of all the world my own.   30

Even now, where Alpine solitudes ascend,
I sit me down a pensive hour to spend;
And, placed on high above the storm's career,
Look downward where an hundred realms appear,
Lakes, forests, cities, plains extending wide,   35
The pomp of kings, the shepherd's humbler pride.

When thus Creation's charms around combine,
Amidst the store, should thankless pride repine?
Say, should the philosophic mind disdain
That good which makes each humbler bosom vain?   40
Let school-taught pride dissemble all it can,
These little things are great to little man;
And wiser he, whose sympathetic mind
Exults in all the good of all mankind.
Ye glittering towns, with wealth and splendour crowned, 45
Ye fields, where summer spreads profusion round,
Ye lakes, whose vessels catch the busy gale,
Ye bending swains, that dress the flowery vale,
For me your tributary stores combine:
Creation's heir, the world, the world is mine!   50

As some lone miser, visiting his store,
Bends at his treasure, counts, re-counts it o'er;
Hoards after hoards his rising raptures fill,
Yet still he sighs, for hoards are wanting still:
Thus to my breast alternate passions rise, 55
Pleased with each good that heaven to man supplies:
Yet oft a sigh prevails, and sorrows fall,
To see the hoard of human bliss so small;
And oft I wish, amidst the scene, to find
Some spot to real happiness consigned, 60
Where my worn soul, each wandering hope at rest,
May gather bliss to see my fellows blest.

But where to find that happiest spot below
Who can direct, when all pretend to know?
The shuddering tenant of the frigid zone 65
Boldly proclaims that happiest spot his own,
Extols the treasures of his stormy seas,
And his long nights of revelry and ease;
The naked negro, panting at the line,
Boasts of his golden sands and palmy wine, 70
Basks in the glare, or stems the tepid wave,
And thanks his gods for all the good they gave.

Such is the patriot's boast, where'er we roam,
His first, best country ever is at home.
And yet, perhaps, if countries we compare, 75
And estimate the blessings which they share,
Though patriots flatter, still shall wisdom find
An equal portion dealt to all mankind;
As different good, by art or nature given,
To different nations makes their blessings even. 80

Nature, a mother kind alike to all,
Still grants her bliss at labour's earnest call;
With food as well the peasant is supplied
On Idra's cliff as Arno's shelvy side;
And though the rocky-crested summits frown,   85
These rocks, by custom, turn to beds of down.
From art more various are the blessings sent;
Wealth, commerce, honour, liberty, content.
Yet these each other's power so strong contest,
That either seems destructive of the rest.   90
Where wealth and freedom reign, contentment fails,
And honour sinks where commerce long prevails.
Hence every state, to one loved blessing prone,
Conforms and models life to that alone.
Each to the favourite happiness attends,   95
And spurns the plan that aims at other ends;
Till, carried to excess in each domain,
This favourite good begets peculiar pain.

But let us try these truths with closer eyes,
And trace them through the prospect as it lies: 100
Here for a while my proper cares resigned,
Here let me sit in sorrow for mankind;
Like yon neglected shrub at random cast,
That shades the steep, and sighs at every blast.

Far to the right, where Apennine ascends,   105
Bright as the summer, Italy extends:
Its uplands sloping deck the mountain's side,
Woods over woods in gay theatric pride;
While oft some temple's mouldering tops between
With venerable grandeur mark the scene.   110

Could Nature's bounty satisfy the breast,
The sons of Italy were surely blest.
Whatever fruits in different climes were found,
That proudly rise, or humbly court the ground;
Whatever blooms in torrid tracts appear, 115
Whose bright succession decks the varied year;
Whatever sweets salute the northern sky
With vernal lives, that blossom but to die;
These here disporting own the kindred soil,
Nor ask luxuriance from the planter's toil; 120
While sea-born gales their gelid wings expand
To winnow fragrance round the smiling land.

But small the bliss that sense alone bestows,
And sensual bliss is all the nation knows.
In florid beauty groves and fields appear, 125
Man seems the only growth that dwindles here.
Contrasted faults through all his manners reign:
Though poor, luxurious; though submissive, vain;
Though grave, yet trifling; zealous, yet untrue;
And even in penance planning sins anew. 130
All evils here contaminate the mind,
That opulence departed leaves behind;
For wealth was theirs, not far removed the date,
When commerce proudly flourished through the state;
At her command the palace learned to rise, 135
Again the long-fallen column sought the skies;
The canvas glowed, beyond even nature warm,
The pregnant quarry teemed with human form;
Till, more unsteady than the southern gale,
Commerce on other shores displayed her sail; 140
While nought remained of all that riches gave,

But towns unmanned, and lords without a slave;
And late the nation found with fruitless skill
Its former strength was but plethoric ill.

Yet still the loss of wealth is here supplied   145
By arts, the splendid wrecks of former pride;
From these the feeble heart and long-fallen mind
An easy compensation seem to find.
Here may be seen, in bloodless pomp arrayed,
The pasteboard triumph and the cavalcade: 150
Processions formed for piety and love,
A mistress or a saint in every grove.
By sports like these are all their cares beguiled;
The sports of children satisfy the child;
Each nobler aim, repressed by long control,   155
Now sinks at last, or feebly mans the soul;
While low delights, succeeding fast behind,
In happier meanness occupy the mind:
As in those domes, where Cæsars once bore sway,
Defaced by time and tottering in decay,   160
There in the ruin, heedless of the dead,
The shelter-seeking peasant builds his shed;
And, wondering man could want the larger pile,
Exults, and owns his cottage with a smile.

My soul, turn from them, turn we to survey   165
Where rougher climes a nobler race display,
Where the bleak Swiss their stormy mansions tread,
And force a churlish soil for scanty bread;
No product here the barren hills afford
But man and steel, the soldier and his sword;   170
No vernal blooms their torpid rocks array,

But winter lingering chills the lap of May;
No zephyr fondly sues the mountain's breast,
But meteors glare, and stormy glooms invest.

   Yet still, even here, content can spread a charm,   175
Redress the clime, and all its rage disarm.
Though poor the peasant's hut, his feasts though small,
He sees his little lot the lot of all;
Sees no contiguous palace rear its head,
To shame the meanness of his humble shed;   180
No costly lord the sumptuous banquet deal,
To make him loathe his vegetable meal;
But calm, and bred in ignorance and toil,
Each wish contracting fits him to the soil.
Cheerful at morn, he wakes from short repose,   185
Breasts the keen air, and carols as he goes;
With patient angle trolls the finny deep;
Or drives his venturous ploughshare to the steep;
Or seeks the den where snow-tracks mark the way,
And drags the struggling savage into day.   190
At night returning, every labour sped,
He sits him down the monarch of a shed;
Smiles by his cheerful fire, and round surveys
His children's looks, that brighten at the blaze;
While his loved partner, boastful of her hoard,   195
Displays her cleanly platter on the board;
And haply too some pilgrim, thither led,
With many a tale repays the nightly bed.

   Thus every good his native wilds impart,
Imprints the patriot passion on his heart;   200
And even those ills that round his mansion rise,

Enhance the bliss his scanty fund supplies.
Dear is that shed to which his soul conforms,
And dear that hill which lifts him to the storms;
And as a child, when scaring sounds molest,   205
Clings close and closer to the mother's breast,
So the loud torrent and the whirlwind's roar
But bind him to his native mountains more.

Such are the charms to barren states assigned;
Their wants but few, their wishes all confined.   210
Yet let them only share the praises due,
If few their wants, their pleasures are but few;
For every want that stimulates the breast
Becomes a source of pleasure when redressed.
Whence from such lands each pleasing science flies,   215
That first excites desires, and then supplies;
Unknown to them, when sensual pleasures cloy,
To fill the languid pause with finer joy;
Unknown those powers that raise the soul to flame,
Catch every nerve and vibrate through the frame.   220
Their level life is but a smouldering fire,
Unquenched by want, unfanned by strong desire;
Unfit for raptures, or, if raptures cheer
On some high festival of once a year,
In wild excess the vulgar breast takes fire,   225
Till, buried in debauch, the bliss expire.

But not their joys alone thus coarsely flow:
Their morals, like their pleasures, are but low;
For, as refinement stops, from sire to son
Unaltered, unimproved, the manners run;   230
And love's and friendship's finely-pointed dart

Fall blunted from each indurated heart.
Some sterner virtues o'er the mountain's breast
May sit, like falcons cowering on the nest;
But all the gentler morals, such as play   235
Through life's more cultured walks, and charm the way,
These, far dispersed, on timorous pinions fly,
To sport and flutter in a kinder sky.

   To kinder skies, where gentler manners reign,
I turn; and France displays her bright domain.   240
Gay, sprightly land of mirth and social ease,
Pleased with thyself, whom all the world can please,
How often have I led thy sportive choir,
With tuneless pipe, beside the murmuring Loire!
Where shading elms along the margin grew,   245
And freshened from the wave the zephyr flew;
And haply, though my harsh touch, faltering still,
But mocked all tune, and marred the dancer's skill,
Yet would the village praise my wondrous power,
And dance, forgetful of the noontide hour.   250
Alike all ages. Dames of ancient days
Have led their children through the mirthful maze,
And the gay grandsire, skilled in gestic lore,
Has frisked beneath the burthen of threescore.

   So blest a life these thoughtless realms display; 255
Thus idly busy rolls their world away:
Theirs are those arts that mind to mind endear,
For honour forms the social temper here.
Honour, that praise which real merit gains,
Or even imaginary worth obtains,   260
Here passes current; paid from hand to hand,

It shifts in splendid traffic round the land :
From courts to camps, to cottages it strays,
And all are taught an avarice of praise.
They please, are pleased, they give to get esteem,   265
Till, seeming blest, they grow to what they seem.

But while this softer art their bliss supplies,
It gives their follies also room to rise ;
For praise too dearly loved, or warmly sought,
Enfeebles all internal strength of thought ;   270
And the weak soul, within itself unblest,
Leans for all pleasure on another's breast.
Hence ostentation here, with tawdry art,
Pants for the vulgar praise which fools impart ;
Here vanity assumes her pert grimace,   275
And trims her robes of frieze with copper lace ;
Here beggar pride defrauds her daily cheer,
To boast one splendid banquet once a year :
The mind still turns where shifting fashion draws,
Nor weighs the solid worth of self-applause.   280

To men of other minds my fancy flies,
Embosomed in the deep where Holland lies.
Methinks her patient sons before me stand,
Where the broad ocean leans against the land ;
And, sedulous to stop the coming tide,   285
Lift the tall rampire's artificial pride.
Onward, methinks, and diligently slow,
The firm connected bulwark seems to grow,
Spreads its long arms amidst the watery roar,
Scoops out an empire, and usurps the shore ;   290
While the pent ocean, rising o'er the pile,

Sees an amphibious world beneath him smile;
The slow canal, the yellow-blossomed vale,
The willow-tufted bank, the gliding sail,
The crowded mart, the cultivated plain— 295
A new creation rescued from his reign.

  Thus, while around the wave-subjected soil
Impels the native to repeated toil,
Industrious habits in each bosom reign,
And industry begets a love of gain. 300
Hence all the good from opulence that springs,
With all those ills superfluous treasure brings,
Are here displayed. Their much-loved wealth imparts
Convenience, plenty, elegance, and arts;
But view them closer, craft and fraud appear, 305
Even liberty itself is bartered here.
At gold's superior charms all freedom flies,
The needy sell it, and the rich man buys.
A land of tyrants, and a den of slaves,
Here wretches seek dishonourable graves, 310
And, calmly bent, to servitude conform,
Dull as their lakes that slumber in the storm.

  Heavens! how unlike their Belgic sires of old!
Rough, poor, content, ungovernably bold;
War in each breast, and freedom on each brow; 315
How much unlike the sons of Britain now!

  Fired at the sound, my genius spreads her wing,
And flies where Britain courts the western spring;
Where lawns extend that scorn Arcadian pride,
And brighter streams than famed Hydaspes glide. 320

There all around the gentlest breezes stray,
There gentle music melts on every spray;
Creation's mildest charms are there combined,
Extremes are only in the master's mind!
Stern o'er each bosom reason holds her state,   325
With daring aims irregularly great,
Pride in their port, defiance in their eye,
I see the lords of human kind pass by;
Intent on high designs, a thoughtful band,
By forms unfashioned, fresh from Nature's hand;   330
Fierce in their native hardiness of soul,
True to imagined right, above control,
While even the peasant boasts these rights to scan,
And learns to venerate himself as man.

Thine, Freedom, thine the blessings pictured here,   335
Thine are those charms that dazzle and endear;
Too blest, indeed, were such without alloy,
But fostered even by freedom, ills annoy:
That independence Britons prize too high,
Keeps man from man, and breaks the social tie;   340
The self-dependent lordlings stand alone,
All claims that bind and sweeten life unknown:
Here, by the bonds of nature feebly held,
Minds combat minds, repelling and repelled;
Ferments arise, imprisoned factions roar,   345
Repressed ambition struggles round her shore,
Till, overwrought, the general system feels
Its motions stopped, or frenzy fire the wheels.

Nor this the worst. As nature's ties decay,
As duty, love, and honour fail to sway,   350

Fictitious bonds, the bonds of wealth and law,
Still gather strength, and force unwilling awe.
Hence all obedience bows to these alone,
And talent sinks, and merit weeps unknown;
Till time may come, when, stripped of all her charms, 355
The land of scholars, and the nurse of arms,
Where noble stems transmit the patriot flame,
Where kings have toiled, and poets wrote for fame,
One sink of level avarice shall lie,
And scholars, soldiers, kings, unhonoured die. 360

Yet, think not, thus when freedom's ills I state,
I mean to flatter kings, or court the great:
Ye powers of truth, that bid my soul aspire,
Far from my bosom drive the low desire!
And thou, fair Freedom, taught alike to feel 365
The rabble's rage, and tyrant's angry steel;
Thou transitory flower, alike undone
By proud contempt or favour's fostering sun,
Still may thy blooms the changeful clime endure!
I only would repress them to secure; 370
For just experience tells, in every soil,
That those who think must govern those that toil;
And all that freedom's highest aims can reach
Is but to lay proportioned loads on each.
Hence, should one order disproportioned grow, 375
Its double weight must ruin all below.

O then how blind to all that truth requires,
Who think it freedom when a part aspires!
Calm is my soul, nor apt to rise in arms,
Except when fast-approaching danger warms; 380
But when contending chiefs blockade the throne,

M. 2

Contracting regal power to stretch their own;
When I behold a factious band agree
To call it freedom when themselves are free;
Each wanton judge new penal statutes draw,   385
Laws grind the poor, and rich men rule the law;
The wealth of climes, where savage nations roam,
Pillaged from slaves to purchase slaves at home;
Fear, pity, justice, indignation start,
Tear off reserve, and bare my swelling heart;   390
Till half a patriot, half a coward grown,
I fly from petty tyrants to the throne.

  Yes, brother, curse with me that baleful hour
When first ambition struck at regal power;
And, thus polluting honour in its source,   395
Gave wealth to sway the mind with double force.
Have we not seen, round Britain's peopled shore,
Her useful sons exchanged for useless ore?
Seen all her triumphs but destruction haste,
Like flaring tapers brightening as they waste?   400
Seen opulence, her grandeur to maintain,
Lead stern depopulation in her train,
And over fields where scattered hamlets rose,
In barren solitary pomp repose?
Have we not seen at pleasure's lordly call   405
The smiling long-frequented village fall?
Beheld the duteous son, the sire decayed,
The modest matron, and the blushing maid,
Forced from their homes, a melancholy train,
To traverse climes beyond the western main;   410
Where wild Oswego spreads her swamps around,
And Niagara stuns with thundering sound?

Even now, perhaps, as there some pilgrim strays
Through tangled forests and through dangerous ways,
Where beasts with man divided empire claim,   415
And the brown Indian marks with murderous aim;
There, while above the giddy tempest flies,
And all around distressful yells arise,
The pensive exile, bending with his woe,
To stop too fearful, and too faint to go,   420
Casts a long look where England's glories shine,
And bids his bosom sympathise with mine.

Vain, very vain, my weary search to find
That bliss which only centres in the mind.
Why have I strayed from pleasure and repose,   425
To seek a good each government bestows?
In every government, though terrors reign,
Though tyrant kings or tyrant laws restrain,
How small, of all that human hearts endure,
That part which laws or kings can cause or cure!   430
Still to ourselves in every place consigned,
Our own felicity we make or find.
With secret course, which no loud storms annoy,
Glides the smooth current of domestic joy.
The lifted axe, the agonizing wheel,   435
Luke's iron crown, and Damiens' bed of steel,
To men remote from power but rarely known,
Leave reason, faith, and conscience, all our own.

THE DESERTED VILLAGE

DEDICATION.

To Sir Joshua Reynolds.

Dear Sir,

I can have no expectations in an address of this kind, either to add to your reputation, or to establish my own. You can gain nothing from my admiration, as I am ignorant of that art in which you are said to excel; and I may lose 5 *much by the severity of your judgment, as few have a juster taste in poetry than you. Setting interest, therefore, aside, to which I never paid much attention, I must be indulged at present in following my affections. The only dedication I ever made was to my brother, because I loved him better* 10 *than most other men. He is since dead. Permit me to inscribe this Poem to you.*

How far you may be pleased with the versification and mere mechanical parts of this attempt, I do not pretend to enquire; but I know you will object (and indeed several of our 15 *best and wisest friends concur in the opinion) that the depopulation it deplores is no where to be seen, and the disorders it laments are only to be found in the poet's own imagination. To this I can scarcely make any other answer than that I sincerely believe what I have written; that I have taken all possible* 20

*pains, in my country excursions, for these four or five years
past, to be certain of what I allege; and that all my views
and enquiries have led me to believe those miseries real, which
I here attempt to display.   But this is not the place to enter*
25 *into an enquiry whether the country be depopulating or not:
the discussion would take up much room, and I should prove
myself, at best, an indifferent politician, to tire the reader with
a long preface, when I want his unfatigued attention to a long
poem.*

30   *In regretting the depopulation of the country, I inveigh
against the increase of our luxuries; and here also I expect
the shout of modern politicians against me.   For twenty or
thirty years past, it has been the fashion to consider luxury as
one of the greatest national advantages; and all the wisdom*
35 *of antiquity in that particular as erroneous.   Still, however,
I must remain a professed ancient on that head, and continue
to think those luxuries prejudicial to states, by which so many
vices are introduced, and so many kingdoms have been undone.
Indeed, so much has been poured out of late on the other side*
40 *of the question, that, merely for the sake of novelty and variety,
one would sometimes wish to be in the right.*

I am, Dear Sir,

Your sincere Friend and ardent Admirer,

OLIVER GOLDSMITH.

THE DESERTED VILLAGE.

Sweet Auburn! loveliest village of the plain,
Where health and plenty cheered the labouring swain,
Where smiling spring its earliest visit paid,
And parting summer's lingering blooms delayed:
Dear lovely bowers of innocence and ease,   5
Seats of my youth, when every sport could please,
How often have I loitered o'er thy green,
Where humble happiness endeared each scene!
How often have I paused on every charm,
The sheltered cot, the cultivated farm,   10
The never-failing brook, the busy mill,
The decent church that topped the neighbouring hill,
The hawthorn bush, with seats beneath the shade,
For talking age and whispering lovers made!
How often have I blessed the coming day,   15
When toil remitting lent its turn to play,
And all the village train, from labour free,
Led up their sports beneath the spreading tree;
While many a pastime circled in the shade,
The young contending as the old surveyed;   20
And many a gambol frolicked o'er the ground,
And sleights of art and feats of strength went round;
And still, as each repeated pleasure tired,
Succeeding sports the mirthful band inspired;

The dancing pair that simply sought renown,   25
By holding out to tire each other down;
The swain mistrustless of his smutted face,
While secret laughter tittered round the place;
The bashful virgin's sidelong looks of love,
The matron's glance that would those looks reprove.   30
These were thy charms, sweet village! sports like these,
With sweet succession, taught even toil to please;
These round thy bowers their cheerful influence shed;
These were thy charms—but all these charms are fled.

Sweet smiling village, loveliest of the lawn,   35
Thy sports are fled, and all thy charms withdrawn;
Amidst thy bowers the tyrant's hand is seen,
And desolation saddens all thy green:
One only master grasps the whole domain,
And half a tillage stints thy smiling plain: 40
No more thy glassy brook reflects the day,
But, choked with sedges, works its weedy way.
Along thy glades, a solitary guest,
The hollow-sounding bittern guards its nest;
Amidst thy desert walks the lapwing flies,   45
And tires their echoes with unvaried cries.
Sunk are thy bowers in shapeless ruin all,
And the long grass o'ertops the mouldering wall;
And, trembling, shrinking from the spoiler's hand,
Far, far away, thy children leave the land.   50

Ill fares the land, to hastening ills a prey,
Where wealth accumulates and men decay:
Princes and lords may flourish, or may fade;
A breath can make them, as a breath has made:

But a bold peasantry, their country's pride,   55
When once destroyed, can never be supplied.

A time there was, ere England's griefs began,
When every rood of ground maintained its man;
For him light labour spread her wholesome store,
Just gave what life required, but gave no more: 60
His best companions, innocence and health;
And his best riches, ignorance of wealth.

But times are altered; trade's unfeeling train
Usurp the land and dispossess the swain;
Along the lawn, where scattered hamlets rose,   65
Unwieldy wealth and cumbrous pomp repose;
And every want to opulence allied,
And every pang that folly pays to pride.
Those gentle hours that plenty bade to bloom,
Those calm desires that asked but little room,   70
Those healthful sports that graced the peaceful scene,
Lived in each look, and brightened all the green;
These, far departing, seek a kinder shore,
And rural mirth and manners are no more.

Sweet Auburn! parent of the blissful hour,   75
Thy glades forlorn confess the tyrant's power.
Here, as I take my solitary rounds,
Amidst thy tangling walks and ruined grounds,
And, many a year elapsed, return to view
Where once the cottage stood, the hawthorn grew,   80
Remembrance wakes with all her busy train,
Swells at my breast, and turns the past to pain.

In all my wanderings round this world of care,
In all my griefs—and God has given my share—

I still had hopes, my latest years to crown,   85
Amidst these humble bowers to lay me down;
To husband out life's taper at the close,
And keep the flame from wasting by repose:
I still had hopes, for pride attends us still,
Amidst the swains to show my book-learned skill,   90
Around my fire an evening group to draw
And tell of all I felt and all I saw;
And as an hare, whom hounds and horns pursue,
Pants to the place from whence at first she flew,
I still had hopes, my long vexations past,   95
Here to return—and die at home at last.

O blest retirement, friend to life's decline,
Retreats from care, that never must be mine,
How happy he who crowns in shades like these
A youth of labour with an age of ease;   100
Who quits a world where strong temptations try,
And, since 't is hard to combat, learns to fly!
For him no wretches, born to work and weep,
Explore the mine, or tempt the dangerous deep;
No surly porter stands in guilty state   105
To spurn imploring famine from the gate;
But on he moves to meet his latter end,
Angels around befriending Virtue's friend;
Bends to the grave with unperceived decay,
While Resignation gently slopes the way;   110
And, all his prospects brightening to the last,
His heaven commences ere the world be past!

Sweet was the sound, when oft at evening's close
Up yonder hill the village murmur rose;

There, as I passed with careless steps and slow,   115
The mingling notes came softened from below;
The swain responsive as the milkmaid sung,
The sober herd that lowed to meet their young,
The noisy geese that gabbled o'er the pool,
The playful children just let loose from school,   120
The watch-dog's voice that bayed the whispering wind,
And the loud laugh that spoke the vacant mind;
These all in sweet confusion sought the shade,
And filled each pause the nightingale had made.
But now the sounds of population fail,   125
No cheerful murmurs fluctuate in the gale,
No busy steps the grass-grown footway tread,
For all the bloomy flush of life is fled.
All but yon widowed, solitary thing,
That feebly bends beside the plashy spring;   130
She, wretched matron, forced in age, for bread,
To strip the brook with mantling cresses spread,
To pick her wintry faggot from the thorn,
To seek her nightly shed, and weep till morn;
She only left of all the harmless train,   135
The sad historian of the pensive plain.

   Near yonder copse, where once the garden smiled,
And still where many a garden flower grows wild;
There, where a few torn shrubs the place disclose,
The village preacher's modest mansion rose.   140
A man he was to all the country dear,
And passing rich with forty pounds a year;
Remote from towns he ran his godly race,
Nor e'er had changed, nor wished to change his place;
Unpractised he to fawn, or seek for power,   145

By doctrines fashioned to the varying hour;
Far other aims his heart had learned to prize,
More skilled to raise the wretched than to rise.
His house was known to all the vagrant train;
He chid their wanderings, but relieved their pain:　150
The long-remembered beggar was his guest,
Whose beard descending swept his aged breast;
The ruined spendthrift, now no longer proud,
Claimed kindred there and had his claims allowed;
The broken soldier, kindly bade to stay,　155
Sat by his fire and talked the night away;
Wept o'er his wounds, or, tales of sorrow done,
Shouldered his crutch, and showed how fields were won.
Pleased with his guests, the good man learned to glow,
And quite forgot their vices in their woe;　160
Careless their merits or their faults to scan,
His pity gave ere charity began.

　Thus to relieve the wretched was his pride,
And even his failings leaned to virtue's side;
But in his duty prompt at every call,　165
He watched and wept, he prayed and felt for all;
And, as a bird each fond endearment tries
To tempt its new-fledged offspring to the skies,
He tried each art, reproved each dull delay,
Allured to brighter worlds, and led the way.　170

　Beside the bed where parting life was laid,
And sorrow, guilt, and pain, by turns dismayed,
The reverend champion stood. At his control
Despair and anguish fled the struggling soul:

Comfort came down the trembling wretch to raise,   175
And his last faltering accents whispered praise.

At church, with meek and unaffected grace,
His looks adorned the venerable place;
Truth from his lips prevailed with double sway,
And fools, who came to scoff, remained to pray.   180
The service past, around the pious man,
With steady zeal, each honest rustic ran;
Even children followed with endearing wile
And plucked his gown, to share the good man's smile.
His ready smile a parent's warmth expressed,   185
Their welfare pleased him, and their cares distressed;
To them his heart, his love, his griefs were given,
But all his serious thoughts had rest in heaven.
As some tall cliff that lifts its awful form,
Swells from the vale and midway leaves the storm,   190
Though round its breast the rolling clouds are spread,
Eternal sunshine settles on its head.

Beside yon straggling fence that skirts the way,
With blossomed furze unprofitably gay,
There, in his noisy mansion, skilled to rule,   195
The village master taught his little school.
A man severe he was and stern to view;
I knew him well, and every truant knew;
Well had the boding tremblers learned to trace
The day's disasters in his morning face;   200
Full well they laughed with counterfeited glee
At all his jokes, for many a joke had he;
Full well the busy whisper, circling round,
Conveyed the dismal tidings when he frowned;
Yet he was kind, or, if severe in aught,   205

The love he bore to learning was in fault.
The village all declared how much he knew;
'T was certain he could write and cipher too;
Lands he could measure, terms and tides presage,
And even the story ran that he could gauge.   210
In arguing, too, the parson owned his skill,
For, even though vanquished, he could argue still;
While words of learned length and thundering sound
Amazed the gazing rustics ranged around;
And still they gazed, and still the wonder grew,   215
That one small head could carry all he knew.

But past is all his fame. The very spot
Where many a time he triumphed, is forgot.
Near yonder thorn, that lifts its head on high,
Where once the sign-post caught the passing eye,   220
Low lies that house where nut-brown draughts inspired,
Where grey-beard mirth and smiling toil retired,
Where village statesmen talked with looks profound,
And news much older than their ale went round.
Imagination fondly stoops to trace   225
The parlour splendours of that festive place;
The white-washed wall, the nicely sanded floor,
The varnished clock that clicked behind the door;
The chest contrived a double debt to pay,
A bed by night, a chest of drawers by day;   230
The pictures placed for ornament and use,
The twelve good rules, the royal game of goose;
The hearth, except when winter chilled the day,
With aspen boughs and flowers and fennel gay;
While broken tea-cups, wisely kept for show,   235
Ranged o'er the chimney, glistened in a row.

Vain transitory splendours! could not all
Reprieve the tottering mansion from its fall?
Obscure it sinks, nor shall it more impart
An hour's importance to the poor man's heart;   240
Thither no more the peasant shall repair
To sweet oblivion of his daily care;
No more the farmer's news, the barber's tale,
No more the woodman's ballad shall prevail;
No more the smith his dusky brow shall clear,   245
Relax his ponderous strength, and lean to hear;
The host himself no longer shall be found
Careful to see the mantling bliss go round;
Nor the coy maid, half willing to be pressed,
Shall kiss the cup to pass it to the rest.   250

Yes! let the rich deride, the proud disdain,
These simple blessings of the lowly train;
To me more dear, congenial to my heart,
One native charm, than all the gloss of art;
Spontaneous joys, where Nature has its play,   255
The soul adopts, and owns their first-born sway;
Lightly they frolic o'er the vacant mind,
Unenvied, unmolested, unconfined.
But the long pomp, the midnight masquerade,
With all the freaks of wanton wealth arrayed,   260
In these, ere triflers half their wish obtain,
The toiling pleasure sickens into pain;
And, even while fashion's brightest arts decoy,
The heart distrusting asks, if this be joy.

Ye friends to truth, ye statesmen, who survey   265
The rich man's joys increase, the poor's decay,

'T is yours to judge how wide the limits stand
Between a splendid and an happy land.
Proud swells the tide with loads of freighted ore,
And shouting Folly hails them from her shore;   270
Hoards even beyond the miser's wish abound,
And rich men flock from all the world around.
Yet count our gains. This wealth is but a name
That leaves our useful products still the same.
Not so the loss. The man of wealth and pride   275
Takes up a space that many poor supplied;
Space for his lake, his park's extended bounds,
Space for his horses, equipage and hounds;
The robe that wraps his limbs in silken sloth
Has robbed the neighbouring fields of half their growth; 280
His seat, where solitary sports are seen,
Indignant spurns the cottage from the green;
Around the world each needful product flies,
For all the luxuries the world supplies;
While thus the land, adorned for pleasure all,   285
In barren splendour feebly waits the fall.

As some fair female, unadorned and plain,
Secure to please while youth confirms her reign,
Slights every borrowed charm that dress supplies,
Nor shares with art the triumph of her eyes;   290
But when those charms are past, for charms are frail,
When time advances, and when lovers fail,
She then shines forth, solicitous to bless,
In all the glaring impotence of dress.
Thus fares the land, by luxury betrayed,   295
In nature's simplest charms at first arrayed;
But verging to decline, its splendours rise,

Its vistas strike, its palaces surprise;
While, scourged by famine, from the smiling land
The mournful peasant leads his humble band;   300
And while he sinks, without one arm to save,
The country blooms—a garden and a grave.

Where then, ah! where shall poverty reside,
To 'scape the pressure of contiguous pride?
If to some common's fenceless limits strayed,   305
He drives his flocks to pick the scanty blade,
Those fenceless fields the sons of wealth divide,
And even the bare-worn common is denied.

If to the city sped—what waits him there?
To see profusion that he must not share;   310
To see ten thousand baneful arts combined
To pamper luxury and thin mankind;
To see each joy the sons of pleasure know
Extorted from his fellow-creature's woe.
Here while the courtier glitters in brocade,   315
There the pale artist plies the sickly trade;
Here while the proud their long-drawn pomps display,
There the black gibbet glooms beside the way.
The dome where Pleasure holds her midnight reign,
Here, richly decked, admits the gorgeous train;   320
Tumultuous grandeur crowds the blazing square,
The rattling chariots clash, the torches glare.
Sure scenes like these no troubles e'er annoy!
Sure these denote one universal joy!
Are these thy serious thoughts?—Ah, turn thine eyes   325
Where the poor houseless shivering female lies.
She once, perhaps, in village plenty blest,

Has wept at tales of innocence distressed;
Her modest looks the cottage might adorn,
Sweet as the primrose peeps beneath the thorn;   330
Now lost to all; her friends, her virtue fled,
Near her betrayer's door she lays her head,
And, pinched with cold, and shrinking from the shower,
With heavy heart deplores that luckless hour,
When idly first, ambitious of the town,   335
She left her wheel and robes of country brown.

   Do thine, sweet Auburn, thine, the loveliest train,
Do thy fair tribes participate her pain?
Even now, perhaps, by cold and hunger led,
At proud men's doors they ask a little bread!   340

   Ah, no. To distant climes, a dreary scene,
Where half the convex world intrudes between,
Through torrid tracts with fainting steps they go,
Where wild Altama murmurs to their woe.
Far different there from all that charmed before,   345
The various terrors of that horrid shore;
Those blazing suns that dart a downward ray,
And fiercely shed intolerable day;
Those matted woods where birds forget to sing,
But silent bats in drowsy clusters cling;   350
Those poisonous fields, with rank luxuriance crowned,
Where the dark scorpion gathers death around;
Where at each step the stranger fears to wake
The rattling terrors of the vengeful snake;
Where crouching tigers wait their hapless prey,   355
And savage men more murderous still than they;
While oft in whirls the mad tornado flies,

Mingling the ravaged landscape with the skies.
Far different these from every former scene,
The cooling brook, the grassy-vested green,   360
The breezy covert of the warbling grove,
That only sheltered thefts of harmless love.

Good Heaven! what sorrows gloomed that parting day,
That called them from their native walks away;
When the poor exiles, every pleasure past,   365
Hung round the bowers, and fondly looked their last,
And took a long farewell, and wished in vain,
For seats like these beyond the western main;
And shuddering still to face the distant deep,
Returned and wept, and still returned to weep!   370
The good old sire the first prepared to go
To new-found worlds, and wept for others' woe;
But for himself, in conscious virtue brave,
He only wished for worlds beyond the grave.
His lovely daughter, lovelier in her tears,   375
The fond companion of his helpless years,
Silent went next, neglectful of her charms,
And left a lover's for a father's arms.
With louder plaints the mother spoke her woes,
And blessed the cot where every pleasure rose,   380
And kissed her thoughtless babes with many a tear,
And clasped them close, in sorrow doubly dear;
Whilst her fond husband strove to lend relief
In all the silent manliness of grief.

O luxury! thou curst by Heaven's decree,   385
How ill exchanged are things like these for thee!
How do thy potions, with insidious joy,

Diffuse their pleasures only to destroy!
Kingdoms by thee, to sickly greatness grown,
Boast of a florid vigour not their own;   390
At every draught more large and large they grow,
A bloated mass of rank unwieldy woe;
Till, sapped their strength, and every part unsound,
Down, down they sink, and spread a ruin round.

   Even now the devastation is begun,   395
And half the business of destruction done;
Even now, methinks, as pondering here I stand,
I see the rural virtues leave the land:
Down where yon anchoring vessel spreads the sail,
That idly waiting flaps with every gale,   400
Downward they move, a melancholy band,
Pass from the shore, and darken all the strand.
Contented toil, and hospitable care,
And kind connubial tenderness are there;
And piety with wishes placed above,   405
And steady loyalty, and faithful love.
And thou, sweet Poetry, thou loveliest maid,
Still first to fly where sensual joys invade;
Unfit, in these degenerate times of shame,
To catch the heart, or strike for honest fame;   410
Dear charming nymph, neglected and decried,
My shame in crowds, my solitary pride;
Thou source of all my bliss, and all my woe,
That found'st me poor at first, and keep'st me so;
Thou guide by which the noble arts excel,   415
Thou nurse of every virtue, fare thee well!
Farewell, and oh! where'er thy voice be tried,
On Torno's cliffs, or Pambamarca's side,

Whether where equinoctial fervours glow,
Or winter wraps the polar world in snow,   420
Still let thy voice, prevailing over time,
Redress the rigours of the inclement clime;
Aid slighted truth with thy persuasive strain;
Teach erring man to spurn the rage of gain;
Teach him, that states of native strength possessed,   425
Though very poor, may still be very blest;
That trade's proud empire hastes to swift decay,
As ocean sweeps the laboured mole away;
While self-dependent power can time defy,
As rocks resist the billows and the sky.   430

NOTES.

THE TRAVELLER.

In the sub-title *prospect* means view, and *society* is used in the wide sense of men grouped in communities, in nations.

DEDICATION.

The Rev. Henry Goldsmith was some six years older than Oliver. A deep affection existed between them, as appears from this dedication, from the opening lines of the poem, and from the dedication of *The Deserted Village*. There Goldsmith says, "The only dedication I ever made was to my brother, because I loved him better than most other men." While most writers dedicated their works to wealthy and noble patrons from whom money or preferment might be got, Goldsmith inscribed *The Traveller* to his brother, *The Deserted Village* to one friend, Sir Joshua Reynolds, and *She Stoops to Conquer* to another, Dr Johnson. In *The Vicar*, ch. xx., Goldsmith satirizes the devices of authors in soliciting permission to dedicate their works to the rich and the influential.

1. **Dear Sir**: such formality to a brother was the usage of the time. In *The Vicar*, ch. x., Sophy addresses her father as "Sir."

7. **Switzerland**: see Introduction, p. xii.

11. **to happiness and obscurity**: this condensed construction of the two nouns with the one verb *retired* is a variety of zeugma. Compare *The Vicar*, ch. xx.: "A gentleman who had just stepped into taste and a large fortune."

forty pounds: the same income as that of the preacher in *The Deserted Village*: see line 142.

18. **what from...and from**: both...and. Compare Chaucer, *Knight's Tale*, 7 sq.:

> "What with his wisdom and his chivalrye,
> He conquered al the regne of Femenye."

In another usage *what* is repeated with the sense of *partly*, especially in the combination *what with*. Compare Carlyle, *Sartor Resartus*, Bk I. ch. i., " What with the labours of our Werners and Huttons, what with the ardent genius of their disciples, it has come about that now, to many a Royal Society, the Creation of a World is little more mysterious than the cooking of a dumpling."

31. **blank verse**, etc.: Dyer, Grainger and others had recently written blank verse; and Gray had written odes in the style of Pindar. Goldsmith, *Polite Literature*, ch. ix., calls several recent poems in blank verse "disagreeable instances of pedantry," and speaks of "the affected security of our odes, the tuneless flow of our blank verse, the pompous epithet, laboured diction, and every other deviation from common sense."

32. **anapests**: this foot consists of two unaccented syllables followed by one accented: as in Campbell, *Lochiel's Warning*, 86,

> "With his back to the field and his feet to the foe."

Goldsmith's *Retaliation* is anapestic.

iambics: see Introduction, p. xv.

alliterative care: Goldsmith does not hunt for "apt alliteration's artful aid," as Churchill calls it, neither does he shun it. See *The Traveller*, 6, 69, 170, 206: *The Deserted Village*, 3, 35, 42, 229.

37. **party**: faction.

45. **half-witted thing**: a contemptuous reference to Charles Churchill, who died shortly before the publication of *The Traveller*. When the Earl of Bute became Prime Minister, many satires were issued against the King, Bute, and the Scotch. One of the fiercest attacks on the Scotch was Churchill's *Prophecy of Famine*.

1—10. Wherever the poet wanders, his heart turns with longing to his brother.

1. The feeling of sadness is brought out not only by the words, but also by the slow movement of the verse.

slow: Goldsmith was once asked if he meant "tardiness of loco-motion," and said yes. Dr Johnson interrupted with the remark:

"No, sir, you do not mean tardiness of locomotion; you mean that sluggishness of mind which comes upon a man in solitude." But Goldsmith undoubtedly did mean slowness of motion. Compare *The Deserted Village*, 115,

"There, as I passed with careless steps and slow."

For the asyndeton here, see note to line 360.

2. **lazy**: the Scheldt is very sluggish.

wandering: the Po has many windings and, when in flood, often bursts its banks.

3. Goldsmith said that once in Carinthia he was driven from a house and forced to spend several hours of the night seeking another shelter.

5. The Roman Campagna has always been unhealthy. In Goldsmith's day it was extremely pestilential and had very few inhabitants.

8. **untravelled**: some critics find a discrepancy between this line and the tenth. But the meaning is that increasing distance from his brother does not lessen his brotherly love. Compare *Citizen of the World*, Letter III., "The farther I travel I feel the pain of separation with stronger force; those ties that bind me to my native country and you are still unbroken. By every remove I only drag a greater length of chain."

11—22. He invokes blessings on his brother, and on his brother's happy and hospitable home.

11. **crown**: subjunctive mood expressing a wish. So *attend* in line 12, and *be* in lines 13, 17.

13. **guests**: has been taken to mean "the long-remembered beggar," "the ruined spendthrift," and "the broken soldier," mentioned as the village preacher's guests, *The Deserted Village*, 151 sqq.; but surely these are referred to in lines 15, 16. Besides, line 14 is not applicable to such vagrants. Understand by *guests*, the inmates, the members of the household.

15. **want and pain**: the needy and the suffering: abstract names used for concrete.

22. **luxury**: unalloyed delight. Note a different meaning in *The Deserted Village*, 385,

"O luxury! thou curst by Heaven's decree."

23—30. It has been the poet's lot to be a homeless wanderer, pursuing a good which he has never secured.

23. **me**: governed by *leads* in line 29.

24. **in wandering spent and care**: note the order of words.

27. **the circle bounding earth and skies**: poetic periphrasis for the horizon.

31—36. Seated on an Alpine crag, he gazes pensively on the scenes below.

34. **an hundred**: a poetic hyperbole.

With this use of *an* before *h* sounded, compare *an hare* in line 93 of *The Deserted Village*. Originally *an* was the only form of the indefinite article, being the Anglo-Saxon *án*, one, with the vowel shortened. In course of time it became usual to put *an* only before vowel sounds: it continued, however, to be frequently used before *h* whether sounded or not. But the usage was far from uniform. Chaucer has *an* before *hare, holy, hundred*. The Authorized Version of the Bible has *an* with *hard, hammer, hireling, helmet*, but *a* with *hen, hole*. Shakespeare has *a* with *horse, husband, hare, hearer*: Addison *an* with *husband, hundred, hereafter*: Burke *an* with *hardy*. Dr Johnson, in the "Grammar" prefixed to his *Dictionary*, 1755, says: "Grammarians of the last age direct that *an* should be used with *h*."

36. **humbler pride**: an example of oxymoron, the adjective being in sharp contrast with the noun. See line 256.

pride: what the shepherd is proud of. Goldsmith uses the word to mean also the state or condition of being proud, haughtiness, noble self-esteem, show, splendour. See lines 38, 41, 108, 146, 277, 286, 319, 327; and *The Deserted Village*, 55, 68, 89, 163, 412.

37—50. Though some in their pride affect to despise these things, the poet's sympathetic mind rejoices in the good of all, and claims a share in it.

39. **philosophic mind**: the disdain of the philosophic mind is, in line 41, called *school-taught pride*, where *school* refers to the mediaeval schools of philosophy and theology. In the first edition, line 39 read, "'Twere affectation all, and school-taught pride."

47. **gale**: a breeze; not a storm or tempestuous wind, as we regularly use the word. The poets often have it in the sense of a gentle breeze, as Shakespeare, *The Tempest*, v. 1. 314,

"Calm seas, auspicious gales."

See *The Traveller*, 121, 139; *The Deserted Village*, 126, 400.

48. **swains**: countrymen, peasants: originally a servant, then a

peasant, and in pastoral poetry a lover: a favourite word in XVIIIth century poetry.

50. **heir**: in apposition to *me* suggested by *mine*, as if it were, "To me, Creation's heir, the world belongs." See note to line 56.

the world is repeated for emphasis.

51—62. Still he grieves that the sum total of happiness is so small. Where can a perfect paradise be found, where in seeing the bliss of others he may himself become happy?

55. **passions**: emotions: see *patriot passion* in line 200. Compare Shakespeare, *King Lear*, v. 3. 198,

"'Twixt two extremes of passion, joy and grief."

56. **pleased**: agrees with *me* suggested by *my* in line 55. Compare *The Deserted Village*, 161, 297.

57. **sorrows**: tears. By the figure of speech called metonymy, the cause is put for the effect.

61. **hope**: nominative absolute. So also in lines 24, 101, 342; *The Deserted Village*, 79, 95, 181, 365, 393.

63—80. But which is the happiest country? Everyone declares his own to be the best. Perhaps the truth is that each country possesses some kind of happiness.

65. **tenant**: inhabitant, native. Gray, *Progress of Poesy*, 57, calls the Arctic regions

"The shivering native's dull abode."

69. **the line**: the equator, as frequently. Note the contrast between 65 and 69.

70. **palmy wine**: palm-wine. A fermented liquor is made from various kinds of palms.

74. **his** is emphatic = for him.

75—80. See Dedication, line 54.

79. **art**: see line 88 for the blessings of art.

81—98. Nature everywhere rewards the peasant's strenuous labour. The gifts of art are most varied, and seem to destroy each other. Every country clings to its peculiar blessing, which is hurtful when pushed to excess.

84. **Idra**: usually taken as the mountain region of Idria, in Carniola, close to Carinthia, which Goldsmith visited in 1755. Speaking in his *Animated Nature*, 1. 51, ed. 1818, of the quicksilver mines of Idria, he calls it Idra. Some, however, identify Idra with Lake Idro in Northern Italy, others with the Greek island Hydra.

shelvy: rising in terraces.

87. **art**: contrasted with nature, as in line 79. The happiness arising from the natural fertility of one country is contrasted with the advantages springing in another from art, that is, human skill as an agent, human workmanship.

90. **either**: properly one or other of two, but here meaning any one of the five blessings mentioned in line 88.

98. **peculiar**: belonging exclusively to one, characteristic. Each good has the defect of its particular excellence.

99—104. To test this theory, the poet resolves to examine the condition of various countries.

100. **prospect**: the scene before him.

101. **my proper**: my own. Compare Shakespeare, *The Tempest*, III. 3. 59 sq.,

> "And even with such-like valour men hang and drown
> Their proper selves."

103. **yon** adds vividness to the description, as if he were writing on the spot. See *The Deserted Village*, 114; and Gray, *Elegy*, 9 sq.,

> "From yonder ivy-mantled tower
> The moping owl does to the moon complain."

105—110. To the right lies the beauteous land of Italy.

105. **Apennine**: usually plural in English. But see Macaulay, *Lake Regillus*, st. II.,

> "O'er purple Apennine";

and Shelley, *Lines written among the Euganean Hills*,

> "The line
> Of the olive-sandalled Apennine."

Compare the Latin "Mons Apenninus."

107, 108. The upland slopes are covered with trees, which rise in tiers like the seats in some splendid theatre. Compare Milton, *Paradise Lost*, IV. 139 sqq.,

> "Cedar and pine and fir and branching palm,
> A sylvan scene; and, as the ranks ascend,
> Shade above shade, a woody theatre
> Of stateliest view."

108. **theatric pride**: a stage metaphor applied to nature. Dr Johnson objected to Gray's

> "O'er Idalia's velvet green" (*Progress of Poesy*, 27)

because nature should not borrow figures from art. But this dictum is disregarded by poets. See the quotation from Shelley in note to line 105; and compare Milton, *Lycidas*, 47

"Frost to flowers, that their gay wardrobe wear."

See *The Deserted Village*, 360.

109. **between**: adverb. So *around* in line 297, and *above* in line 417.

111—122. Italy possesses all the gifts of nature in abundance.

112. **were**: past subjunctive, indicating a purely imaginary supposition of the present.

113. **climes**: regions, as in line 410. In line 369 it means climate.

were: the reading of the 9th edition, 1774, has been changed by some editors to *are*, to make it agree in tense with the other verbs. The meaning of *are found* will then be simply "grow, appear, occur." But we may keep *were* and explain it as "were found and brought to Italy." The elder Pliny, *Natural History*, xv. 25, mentions that Lucullus introduced the cherry-tree from Cerasus in Pontus. Other fruit-trees acclimatized in Italy are the citron, the peach, the orange, and the date-palm.

114. **rise...court**: presents indicating a universal truth, and consequently used quite properly with the past tense in 113. Compare Southey, *Roderick*, x. 48 sqq.

"When the stars were setting, at what hour
The breath of heaven is coldest, they beheld
Within a lonely grove the expected fire."

115. **blooms**: strictly blossoms, here used figuratively for flowers in brilliant bloom. The poet speaks of the brilliance of the tropical flowers, and of the fragrance of those of more northerly latitudes.

116. **varied**: proleptic use of adjective; that is, the year is by anticipation called varied, though it becomes varied only through the action expressed by the verb.

120. **luxuriance**: abundant and vigorous growth. The plants, growing freely and luxuriantly, need little of the gardener's care, and show that the soil is naturally suitable to them.

Compare "rank luxuriance" in *The Deserted Village*, 351.

121. **gelid**: properly means extremely cold, but the context suggests cooling sea-breezes.

122. **winnow**: scatter, diffuse. The metaphor is from winnowing corn, separating the chaff from the grain by means of the wind.

smiling: gay, joyous. Goldsmith is fond of this metaphorical use of *smile*=to be gay (with flowers, fruit, &c.), to be happy (through any kind of prosperity). Compare 292, 406; and *The Deserted Village*, 3, 35, 40, 137, 299.

123—144. The Italians, however, have degenerated. They have lost their commerce, but they retain its evils.

124. **sensual**: coming from any of the five senses.

125. **florid**: bright with the rich colouring of flowers and trees.

127. **manners**: see note to line 228.

133 sqq. In the Middle Ages Italian commerce was very flourishing. Favourably situated in the middle of the Mediterranean, Italy commanded the trade between the east and the west. Genoa and Venice were particularly famous and wealthy. The discovery of America and of the Cape route to India helped to transfer commercial supremacy to other countries.

135—138. The wealthy states encouraged architecture, painting, and sculpture.

Compare Thomson, *Autumn*, 134 sqq.

> "Then too the pillared dome, magnific, heaved
> Its ample roof;   .   .   .   .   .   .
> .   .   .   .   . the canvas smooth,
> With glowing life protuberant, to the view
> Embodied rose; the statue seemed to breathe,
> And soften into flesh beneath the touch
> Of forming art, imagination-flushed."

142. **unmanned**: without inhabitants. The usual meaning is rendered effeminate.

143. **skill**: knowledge. The knowledge came too late, and so was useless.

144. **plethoric ill**: it is Dr Goldsmith the physician who speaks. He compares the state of Italy to that of a man suffering from plethora, when the vessels are over-charged with humours, and stoutness is a symptom not of good health but of disease. Compare *The Deserted Village*, 389—394, which amplifies what is said here.

145—164. True, art gives compensation, but it too has degenerated. Nobler aims now gone, the Italians find pleasure in low delights.

146. **arts**: as in 304, the Fine Arts, sculpture, painting, &c.

147. **long-fallen**: they have long lost their high aspirations.

149. **bloodless**: celebrating no blood-won victory.

156. **mans**: animates, braces up.

159. **domes**: palaces.

Caesars: Roman Emperors. The proper name has become a title. Compare Byron, *Manfred*, III. 4,

> "From out the Caesars' palace came
> The owl's long cry."

This word gave to Anglo-Saxon the form *cásere*, and to middle English the form *keysar*, both meaning Emperor. So still in German, *Kaiser*, and in Russian, *Czar*.

162. **shed**: the *cottage* of line 164. So *hut* in line 177 is *shed* in line 180.

165—174. Let us now turn to Switzerland, with its bleak hills and stormy climate, but sturdy inhabitants.

With the whole passage on Switzerland, compare Wordsworth, *Descriptive Sketches*.

165. **turn**: the first occurrence is imperative, 2nd sing.: the second is present subjunctive, 1st plur., hortative use.

167. **bleak**: bare, ungenial, cheerless. The epithet belongs to the country but is here transferred to the inhabitants.

mansions: the Swiss mountains, as in line 201. The word, which is derived from Old French *mansion*, from Latin *mansion-em*, meant originally dwelling. Milton applies it to Eden, *Paradise Lost*, VIII. 296; Gray, to the human body, *Elegy*, 42; Pope to bird's nests, *Odyssey*, V. 85; and Goldsmith, *Animated Nature*, II. 272, to a squirrel's nest. See also *The Deserted Village*, 140.

170. The second half of the line repeats the first, but in more specific terms. Swiss mercenaries served in many armies, especially in the French and the Italian. It has been calculated that from about 1450 to about 1750, over 1,000,000 of them served France. Compare Shakespeare, *Hamlet*, IV. 5. 97,

> "Where are my Switzers? Let them guard the door."

172. **lap**: poetic metaphor for the middle of May. Compare *skirt* for the extreme parts, as Shakespeare, *As You Like It*, III. 2. 353, "In the skirts of the forest, like fringe upon a petticoat."

173. **zephyr**: the west wind: used also of any gentle soft wind. Compare line 246. The word is from French *zephyr*, from Latin *zephyrus*, from Greek ζέφυρος.

M. 4

175—198. Contentment is the compensation of the Swiss. None envies his neighbour. Their wishes are all restricted. Cheerful toil is followed by well-earned rest.

176. Compare *The Deserted Village*, 422,

> "Redress the rigours of the inclement clime."

179. **contiguous**: neighbouring, close at hand.

181. **costly**: lavish in expenditure, extravagant.

deal: distribute: compare line 78. The verb is derived from the noun, which in Anglo-Saxon is *dǽl*, portion, share—a meaning still found in various dialects: see *English Dialect Dictionary*. *Dole* is a doublet of *deal*.

184. **contracting**: shrinking, growing small: used intransitively. *Wish* is subject to *fits*; and *him* is qualified by *calm* and *bred*.

186. **carols**: sings merrily.

187. **patient angle**: epithet transferred from the angler to his angle, which Dr Johnson defines as "an instrument to take fish, consisting of a rod, a line, and a hook." Anglo-Saxon *angul*, fishing-hook, Dutch and German, *angel*. Latin *uncus* is cognate.

Compare Pope, *Windsor Forest*, 137 sq.:

> "The patient fisher takes his silent stand,
> Intent, his angle trembling in his hand."

trolls: fishes for pike. The word means generally to roll, but as a fishing term "to fish for pike with a rod the line of which runs on a reel."

finny deep: note the bold figure of speech. Pope, *Odyssey*, IV. 528, has "fishy flood," that is, abounding in fish; *Rape of the Lock*, II. 26, "finny prey"; and, *Windsor Forest*, 139, "scaly breed." But here the water is called *finny* as containing creatures with fins. "Warbling grove," *The Deserted Village*, 361, has been suggested as a parallel.

188. Boldly drives his plough close to the brink of a precipice.

190. **savage**: bear or wolf. As the bear hibernates, perhaps *snow-tracks* in line 189 favours the wolf. *Savage* as a noun is now restricted to human beings. Thomson uses it for wolves, *Winter*, 401; and Pope for a boar, *Iliad*, XVII. 814.

191. **sped**: finished, completed.

191—196. With this domestic scene, compare Burns, *Cotter's Saturday Night*, st. 3.

192. **sits him**: note *him* used reflexively, in the objective case

with an intransitive verb. So in line 32. Compare Shakespeare, *Antony and Cleopatra*, IV. 7. 16,

> "Come thee on."

This usage, originally a dative case, is regularly found in Anglo-Saxon and Middle English with intransitive verbs of motion.

196. **cleanly:** means the habit of being clean rather than the actual state. The same contrast is found between *drunken* and *drunk*; *taciturn* and *silent*.

197. **pilgrim:** traveller, wanderer.

197, 198. One of Goldsmith's own experiences.

198. **nightly:** for the night. The word now usually means every night.

199—208. The very hardships enhance the happiness enjoyed by the Swiss, and the wildness of the country only makes it dearer to them.

200. **patriot passion:** patriotism, *the patriot flame* of line 357.

passion: zealous, ardent love. Compare line 55.

203. Note the effective inversion by which the adjective complement of the predicate comes first. Compare *The Deserted Village*, 113. So Shakespeare, *As You Like It*, II. 1. 12,

> "Sweet are the uses of adversity";

and Tennyson, *Lotos Eaters*, *Choric Song*, st. VI.,

> "Dear is the memory of our wedded lives,
> And dear the last embraces of our wives."

206. **close and closer:** the comparative inflection is expressed only once. Compare Burns, *Tam o' Shanter*, 100,

> "Near and more near the thunders roll."

209—226. Still, their pleasures are few and lack refinement.

215. **science:** the word here has not the restricted sense now usually given to it. "Pleasing science" is what produces the "finer joy" (line 218), and is one of the "powers" (line 219), namely, music, poetry, etc. The art of the minstrel or troubadour was called the "Gay or Joyous Science": Scott, *Fair Maid of Perth*, ch. xi. Gray uses *science* for knowledge generally, *Elegy*, 119.

216. **supplies:** gratifies the desire.

221. **level:** of even tenor, monotonous.

224. **of once a year:** yearly, annual. The phrase *once a year* is adverbial, as in line 278, but here *once* is governed by *of* as if it were a substantive, and the new phrase becomes adjectival.

226. expire : see note to line 112 of *The Deserted Village*.

227—238. Their manners too are low. Culture must find a home elsewhere.

228. morals : the word does not refer here to virtue and vice, but is the same as *manners* in line 230; that is, not ceremonious behaviour, but habits, general way of life. So in line 235 *gentler morals* are the refined habits of men of culture, called *gentler manners* in line 239. Compare line 127.

231, 232. Note *fall* plural though only a singular subject *dart* is expressed. According to English idiom *dart* is to be supplied after *love's*, for the sign of the possessive with each noun indicates that there are two darts. Compare *The Vicar*, ch. xviii., "Dryden's and Rowe's manner are quite out of fashion." Contrast the following where there is only one "return" : Shakespeare, *Merchant of Venice*, III. 4. 30,

"Until her husband and my lord's return."

The same construction in Scott, *Ivanhoe*, ch. xxx. : "the blasphemer and parricide's deathbed," indicates that one and the same person is meant.

232. indurated : hardened.

239—254. Yes, France is the home of gentler manners—France, where, says the poet, the villagers often danced gaily to the music of his flute.

239. to kinder skies : the repetition of the closing words of the last paragraph makes an easy transition from one country to another. Compare lines 165, 281, 316, for other transitions.

241. social : of, or belonging to, society; that is, men living in a community for fellowship and mutual help. Burns, *To a Mouse*, 8, speaks of "nature's social union," the state when men and animals lived in friendship and not at war.

243—254. A fragment of Goldsmith's own wanderings. Compare George Primrose in *The Vicar*, ch. xx. : "I passed among the harmless peasants of Flanders, and among such of the French as were poor enough to be very merry; for I ever found them sprightly in proportion to their wants. Whenever I approached a peasant's house towards nightfall, I played one of my most merry tunes, and that procured me not only a lodging, but subsistence for the next day."

243. sportive choir : merry band of dancers : a rare meaning in English. The Greek χορός, from which through Latin *chorus* and Old

French *cuer* the word came, means dance in a ring, band of dancers. The older forms of the word began with *qu-*, as *quire*, which gives the pronunciation much better than *choir*, a spelling modelled on Latin *chorus* or French *chœur*. The rhyming of *choir* with *Loire* is faulty, unless Goldsmith pronounced them differently from what is common to-day. In some districts (see *New English Dictionary*) *choir* is pronounced not as *quire* but as *coir*. If Goldsmith did so, and if he pronounced *Loire* similarly, the rhyme will do. The French *oi* was so pronounced in English, as may be seen in such passages as Shakespeare, *Richard II.*, v. 3. 119 sq.:

"Speak it in French, king; say pardonne moi."
Dost thou teach pardon pardon to destroy?"

But it is difficult to understand how Goldsmith with his acquaintance with French could have admitted such a rhyme.

244. **pipe**: flute. Goldsmith's flute-playing is often mentioned; and we must not take *tuneless* literally, nor yet the other depreciatory remark in 247 sq.

246. **wave**: water, as often in poetry.

249. **village**: villagers; by the figure of metonymy the container is used for the contained.

250. **noontide hour**: hour of noon. *Tide* here means time, as in compounds like *Whitsuntide*. See *The Deserted Village*, 209.

251. **all ages**: old and young.

dames of ancient days: poetic periphrasis for grandams, old women.

252. **mirthful maze**: joyous dance. *Maze* indicates the winding and turning of the dancers.

253. **gestic lore**: the art of dancing. *Gestic* means pertaining to movements of the body. Compare *gesture* and *gesticulate*. Scott, *Peveril of the Peak*, ch. xxx., uses "gestic art" to describe Fenella's dancing before Charles II.

254. Skipped like a lamb though he carried the load of sixty years on his back.

burthen: this spelling, now unusual, is the original: Anglo-Saxon *byrðen*. The spelling with *d* was helped by the existence of *burden*, refrain of a song.

255—266. In France honour is the chief aim: praise, deserved or not, is current coin. All please and are pleased. They seem happy, and at last grow to be happy.

256. **idly busy** : busy about trifles. See note to line 36.

Compare "idle industry," *The Vicar*, ch. xxvii.; Scott, *Marmion*, IV., Introduction, 51 sq. :

> " Or idly busied him to guide
>
>   His angle o'er the lessened tide " ;

and Horace, *Epistles* I. xi. 28,

> " Strenua nos exercet inertia,"

which Martin translates

> " Ever-busy idlers that we are."

257. **arts** : acts of courtesy and complaisance, compliments, and flattery. Compare line 267.

Hazlitt, in the *Plain Speaker*, says of the French : " They split on this rock of complaisance, surrendering every principle to the fear of giving offence, as we do on the opposite one of party-spirit and rancorous hostility."

258. The spirit that pervades the French is to stand well in each other's eyes.

267—280. But this greed of praise makes the French lose independence of soul, and use unworthy means to obtain praise.

273. **ostentation** : abstract for concrete, and personification. So *vanity* in line 275, and *pride* in line 277.

tawdry : showy and without taste. The *t* is the last letter of *Saint*, for the word stands for St Awdry, St Etheldreda. The present meaning arose from cheap finery sold at St Awdry's Fair.

276. Instead of rich material, vanity must be content with frieze, a coarse woollen with shaggy nap ; trimmed also with copper lace instead of gold.

277. These poor proud people give their friends a grand banquet once a year, and starve themselves all the rest of the year.

cheer : food, so called because it gladdens. The word is from Old French *chiere* or *chere*, from Latin *cara*, both meaning face. In English it meant face at first : then mien, look, state of mind, gladness.

279 sq. Compare what Addison says about " the solid worth of self-applause," *Spectator*, No. 122, " A man's first care should be to avoid the reproaches of his own heart ; his next, to escape the censures of the world : if the last interferes with the former, it ought to be entirely neglected ; but otherwise there cannot be a greater satisfaction

to an honest mind, than to see those approbations which it gives itself seconded by the applauses of the public."

281—296. In imagination, the poet now views Holland, with its patient inhabitants, who have won their land from the sea.

281. **my fancy flies**: because, though he could view Italy, Switzerland, and France from his Alpine seat, he could see Holland only with his mind's eye.

284. **leans against the land**: at high tide there may be a difference of twenty-five feet or more in the level of the land and of the ocean washing the protecting dykes. With this passage, compare *Animated Nature*, I. 160, " We find that the whole republic of Holland seems to be a conquest upon the sea, and in a manner rescued from its bosom. The surface of the earth, in this country, is below the level of the bed of the sea ; and I remember, upon approaching the coast, to have looked down upon it from the sea, as into a valley."

285. **sedulous**: assiduous, patiently and perseveringly industrious.

286. **rampire**: dyke, called *bulwark* in line 288. *Rampire* is another form of *rampart*, just as French *rempart* was formerly *rempar*, the more correct form, the *t* being excrescent. Compare Coryat (quoted in *New English Dictionary*), " A strong Rampier betwixt the Adriatique sea and the citie."

290. This is the literal truth. Much of Holland has been wrested from the sea. Compare the old Dutch proverb, " God made the sea, but the Hollander made the land"; and the motto of the province of Zealand, " Luctor et emergo."

291. **pent**: usually means cooped up, but the ocean was shut out. Goldsmith speaks as if the sea felt straitened by the dyke.

292. **amphibious**: being a country of land and water : see the next lines.

293 sqq. Note the succession of balanced phrases consisting of nouns and attributes.

Goldsmith has omitted one conspicuous feature of a Dutch landscape—the windmill.

297—312. Their industry has made them lovers of gain. They possess all the advantages of wealth, and all its disadvantages. Freedom even is bought and sold.

297. **around**: adverb. See line 109.

303. **are** : plural predicate with singular subject *the good* followed by *with all those ills*.

Compare 1 Chronicles xxv. 9, "Gedaliah, who with his brethren and sons were twelve"; and in Latin, Livy, XXI. 60, "Ipse dux cum aliquot principibus capiuntur." Some authorities refuse to admit this construction except in sentences like "The man with his dog is crossing the bridge," or, "The general was captured with his staff," where the *with* phrase is regarded as an adjunct of the singular subject. Where both nouns express co-ordinate ideas, these authorities would not say, "The soldier with his two comrades were killed," but, "The soldier and his two comrades were killed."

309. Compare *Citizen of the World*, Letter XXXV., where it is said of Persia, "A nation, famous for setting the world an example of freedom, is now become a land of tyrants and a den of slaves."

313—316. How unlike the Dutch are to the ancient Belgae and to the modern British !

312. The lakes of Holland did not all "slumber in the storm"; for Haarlem Lake, now drained, frequently rose during storms to an alarming height and caused much damage.

313. The ancestors of the Dutch were Batavian and Frisian rather than Belgic. Compare Scott, *Marmion*, III. Introduction, 129 sqq., who says of the Dutch in the East Indies,

> "Look east, and ask the Belgian why,
> Beneath Batavia's sultry sky
> He seeks not eager to inhale
> The freshness of the mountain gale?"

The objection to-day to this use of "Belgic" and "Belgian" is that Belgium is what it was not when Goldsmith and Scott were writing— an independent sovereign state. Accordingly "Belgic" means belonging to Belgium, as distinct from Holland, or any other state.

314, 315. Goldsmith has in mind Caesar's account of the Nervii, one division of the Belgae : *De Bello Gallico*, II. 15 sqq.

316. Several editors remark on the weakness of this transition. See line 239.

317—334. Reason rules the British. Proud and courageous, they are intent on lofty aims, tenacious of their rights, and lovers of liberty.

Note this eulogy of Britain.

317. **her wing**: *genius* personified is regularly masculine in English. Perhaps Goldsmith was thinking of his muse, his poetic fancy, and so used *her wing*. See note to line 411.

319. **lawns**: glades, grassy clearings in a wood. The word is from Old French *lande*, open ground, heath, and even as late as XVIIIth century was sometimes spelt *laund*. The present day meaning is comparatively recent.

Arcadian pride: Arcadia, in reality the Switzerland of Greece, became with the poets the ideal land of pastoral beauty and rustic simplicity.

320. **famed Hydaspes**: the Jhelum, a tributary of the Indus and one of the five rivers of the Punjab. Many romantic stories clustered round this river. Compare Horace, *Odes*, I. xxii. 7 sq.,

> "Quae loca fabulosus
> Lambit Hydaspes."

322. Refers to the warbling of birds.

324. The extremes are not in the climate but in the minds of the inhabitants.

330. **by forms unfashioned**: unconventional, not formal.

332. **imagined**: does not mean imaginary, visionary, but what they conceive to be theirs.

333. **boasts**: proudly exults in his claim to scrutinize those rights.

335—348. But the very independence of the British produces fierce factions in public life and destroys the sweetness of social intercourse.

335 sq. Note the apostrophe. Freedom was a favourite subject in the XVIIIth century. Compare Cowper, *The Task*, v. 446 sqq., and Addison, *Letter from Italy*,

> "Thee, goddess, thee Britannia's isle adores:
> *   *   *   *   *
> 'Tis liberty that crowns Britannia's isle,
> And makes her barren rocks and her bleak mountains smile."

See *The Vicar*, ch. xix., where Dr Primrose, charged with being an enemy of liberty, says ironically, "I am for liberty! that attribute of the gods! Glorious liberty! that theme of modern declamation! I would have all men kings! I would be a king myself."

339 sqq. See Hazlitt quoted in note to line 257.

340. **social tie**: that which binds men in communities for mutual

help. So *bonds of nature* in line 343; and *nature's ties* in line 349, which in the first edition had *social bonds.*

341. **self-dependent** : depending on none but himself. Contrast line 272.

lordlings : each acts like a little lord.

345. Political feeling ran very high about this time. See Lecky, *England in the XVIIIth Century*, vol. III., ed. 1882; or Macaulay, *Essay on Chatham.*

imprisoned : is explained as hemmed in by the sea. In line 343, the first edition had,

"See, though by circling deeps together held,"
which distinctly refers to the insular position of Britain. Some editors explain *bonds of nature*—the present reading—as the encircling ocean.

347. **the general system** : the state, the body politic.

348. **wheels** : of the machinery, to which metaphorically the state is compared.

349—360. Wealth and law exercise undue influence. Talent sinks, and merit is not recognized. This may end in reducing all to one dead level.

349—351. Nature's ties, namely, duty, love, honour, are contrasted with the fictitious, that is, artificial bonds of wealth and law.

Note that *fictitious* has not its usual meaning of unreal, feigned.

358. **wrote** : frequently found in XVIIIth century for *written.* Gray's *Elegy* in the first edition was entitled *Elegy wrote in a Country Churchyard.* Goldsmith uses both forms.

359. The degrading influence of greed will bring all down to a low level.

360. **scholars, soldiers, kings** : note the absence of conjunctions where they might have been expected. This figure, called asyndeton, gives energy and vividness. Compare lines 1, 35, 88, 293 sqq., 314, 389; *The Deserted Village*, 10 sqq., 187, 258. The opposite figure is polysyndeton, that is, a redundancy of conjunctions, which adds emphasis by individualizing each particular. See lines 353, 354, and *The Deserted Village*, 21 sqq., 234, 366 sqq., 380 sqq., 403 sqq. Compare a famous instance, Romans viii. 38 sq. The ordinary English usage, with three or more particulars, is well exemplified in line 304,

"Convenience, plenty, elegance, and arts."
Compare 438; *The Deserted Village*, 169 sq., 245 sq.

361—376. The poet is a lover of liberty, which unhappily is injured equally by mobs and by tyrants. Experience shows that the thinkers should rule the toilers, and that each class should bear its own share of public burdens.

362. **the great**: frequently used for the rich, the powerful, those eminent in rank and position. Compare Gray, *Progress of Poesy*, 123,
"Beneath the Good how far—but far above the Great."

366. Illustrations of the injury to liberty by "tyrant" and "rabble" will be found in volume III. of Lecky's *History*, cited in note to line 345. Compare the French Revolution and the Napoleon Despotism.

angry steel. Note the double figure of speech—the transferred epithet *angry*; and the material *steel* used for the weapon: synecdoche.

370. The luxuriant growth of liberty must be checked to secure its permanence.

377—392. It is not freedom when only one order is free. Here we have factions striving to diminish the royal power, and the rich ruling the law. The poet flies to the king for safety.

378. **a part aspires**: one order in the state grows too strong and upsets the balance. Compare line 375. Contrast this use of *aspires* with that in line 363, where it means to have high aspirations, desires for what is noble.

381. **contending chiefs**: leaders of rival factions. Lecky (vol. III. p. 20) quotes Lord Melcombe as saying that certain great families "have taken the sole direction of the royal interest and influence into their own hands and applied it to their own creatures without consulting the Crown or leaving room for the royal nomination or direction."

382. Compare *The Vicar*, ch. xix., "It is the interest of the great, therefore, to diminish kingly power as much as possible; because, whatever they take from that is naturally restored to themselves." During the reigns of George I. and George II. the Whigs had acquired immense power: George II. once remarked, "Ministers are the King in this country." To break the power of the Whig nobles was George III.'s aim: more than once he declared he would not be "shackled by those desperate men." See Histories; for example, Green's *Short History*, chs. ix. and x.

385. **wanton**: unrestrained by principles of justice, acting capriciously. At this time there were frequent complaints against magistrates and judges.

new penal statutes: penal laws, especially those involving capital punishment, were largely increased in the XVIIIth century. See *The Vicar*, ch. xxvii., "All our possessions are paled up with new edicts every day, and hung round with gibbets to scare every invader." Compare *The Deserted Village*, 318.

387, 388. A reference to the purchase of seats in Parliament by Nabobs. Lecky (vol. III. p. 171) says: "In the first decade of George III. also, the Nabobs, or Indian adventurers, who had returned in great numbers laden with the spoils of Hindostan, began to appear prominently in English political life. At the end of 1767, Chesterfield, being desirous of bringing his son into Parliament, offered a borough-monger £2500 for a secure seat, but was told that there was no such thing as a borough to be had now, for that the rich East and West Indians had secured them all at the rate of £3000 at least." Of the extortion of the East India Company's servants, Lecky says (pp. 474, 477) the natives had never experienced a tyranny so skilful, so searching and so strong. "The current price of boroughs," says Belsham in his history, vol. v. p. 268, "was enormously raised by the rival plunderers of the East and the West, who by a new species of alchymy had transmuted into English gold the Blood of Africa and the Tears of Hindostan." Clive set himself to cultivate Parliamentary interest, and purchased property to have safe seats for his supporters. See Macaulay's *Clive*, where occurs a famous description of the Nabobs.

392. At that time many thinkers believed that the only hope of escape from aristocratic absolutism ("petty tyrants") lay in absolute monarchy. This view appears in Churchill's *Farewell*, 363 sqq.:

> "Let not a Mob of Tyrants seize the helm,
> Nor titled upstarts league to rob the realm:
>   *   *   *   *   *   *   *
> If, all too short, our course of Freedom run,
> 'Tis thy good pleasure we should be undone,
> Let us, some comfort in our griefs to bring,
> Be slaves to one, and be that one a King."

393—412. It was indeed a calamitous time when the royal power was first shaken. The rich became more powerful; and, to maintain their grandeur, they are now depopulating the country, and forcing the inhabitants to emigrate.

393. baleful: pernicious, full of malign influence. *Bale*, evil, harm, is from Anglo-Saxon *bealu*.

395. its source: the king.

396. gave: permitted.

397 sqq. See Introduction, p. xiii. Compare *The Deserted Village*, 37 sqq., 63 sqq., 265 sqq. Note the figure of Interrogation where, by means of a question, an emphatic assertion is made.

398. Not that they are sold as slaves, but the influx of wealth makes its possessors wish to have spacious parks round their mansions. For this purpose, they evict the villagers, who are forced to emigrate.

Note the sharp antithesis of *useful* and *useless*. Goldsmith makes a similar remark about projects to colonize the new British possessions in America: *Citizen of the World*, Letter XVII.: "And what are the commodities which this colony, when established, is to produce in return? Why, raw silk, hemp, and tobacco. England, therefore, must make an exchange of her best and bravest subjects for raw silk, hemp, and tobacco; her hardy veterans and honest tradesmen must be trucked for a box of snuff or a silk petticoat. Strange absurdity!"

407 sqq. The departure of emigrants is most fully pictured in *The Deserted Village*, 363 sqq.

407. duteous son...sire decayed: the figure of chiasmus, literally "crossing," where in balanced phrases or clauses the order of the first is inverted in the second. Compare line 420; and Cowley, *A Wish*,

> "This only grant me, that my means may lie
> Too low for envy, for contempt too high."

409. train: company, band. See note to line 17 of *The Deserted Village*.

410. western main: the Atlantic Ocean. See *The Deserted Village*, 341, 368.

411. Oswego: a river flowing into Lake Ontario, and well known in Goldsmith's time. Forts Oswego and Niagara figured in the wars in America, 1756 and following years. In English, rivers personified are usually masculine, but Oswego is here made feminine. See note to line 317.

412. Niagara: here accented on the third syllable, *Niagára*, the original accentuation. We have a similar shifting of accent in *Trafalgar*, which Scott and Byron accent differently from modern usage. See *Childe Harold*, IV. st. 181,

"Alike the Armada's pride or spoils of Trafalgar";

and *Marmion*, I., Introduction, 82,

"On Egypt, Hafnia, Trafalgar."

with thundering sound: the name *Niagara* means thunder of waters.

411, 412. Note the use of sonorous names. Compare Scott, *Marmion*, III. st. 9,

"On Susquehanna's swampy ground,
Kentucky's wood-encumbered brake,
Or wild Ontario's boundless lake,
Where heart-sick exiles, in the strain,
Recalled fair Scotland's hills again!"

The skilful use of proper names is regarded as characteristic of the greatest poets; and the following passage from Milton's *Lycidas*, 160 sqq., is often cited as a striking example:

"Sleep'st by the fable of Bellerus old,
Where the great Vision of the guarded mount
Looks towards Namancos and Bayona's hold."

413—422. Perhaps some of those exiles, amid the horrors of American forests, are even now casting looks of regret towards England, as the poet himself is doing. With this paragraph compare *The Deserted Village*, 341 sqq.

416. brown Indian: the American Indian is usually called Red, but brown is equally suitable for a complexion reddish, coppery or cinnamon in colour. The aborigines of America, named Indians by mistake, are regarded by most authorities as belonging, like the Chinese and the Japanese, to the yellow Mongolic race.

417. Compare *The Deserted Village*, 357,

"While oft in whirls the mad tornado flies."

giddy: whirling with bewildering rapidity.

418. distressful: causing distress.

419. pensive: filled with gloomy thoughts.

420. Written by Dr Johnson. So also 429—434, and 437, 438.

422. Goldsmith on his travels had looked back with longing to his native land, and he feels that "heart-sick" exiles do the same. Compare quotation from Scott, note to 411, 412.

423 *to end*. The search for happiness is vain. Happiness is not caused by the kind of government, but lies in ourselves, in our qualities of mind and character.

424. Compare Milton, *Paradise Lost*, I. 254 sq.:

"The mind is its own place, and in itself
Can make a heaven of hell, a hell of heaven";

and Horace, *Epistles*, I. xi. 25 sqq.:

"Nam si ratio et prudentia curas,
Non locus effusi late maris arbiter aufert,
Caelum, non animum, mutant qui trans mare currunt.
Strenua nos exercet inertia; navibus atque
Quadrigis petimus bene vivere. Quod petis hic est,
Est Ulubris, animus si te non deficit aequus."

429, 430. The French peasants of 1764, the Sicilian subjects of King Bomba in 1848, and the Russians of to-day, would hardly agree with this couplet.

435. **lifted**: note the graphic touch produced by the epithet, which describes the most exciting moment of an execution. Compare Browning, *Easter Day*, st. XXX.:

"The form, I looked to have stirred
With pity and approval, rose
O'er me, as when the headsman throws
Axe over shoulder to make end."

agonizing wheel: a barbarous method of capital punishment—well called *agonizing*, causing intense agony. It was common in France and Germany, where the criminal was fixed on a wheel, arms and legs extending along the spokes. As the wheel turned, his limbs were broken by blows with an iron bar.

436. **Luke's iron crown**: Luke was one of two brothers, Dosa, who headed a revolt of the Hungarian peasants in 1514. The other brother, George, was chosen king; and, when the rising was crushed, he was punished by having a red-hot crown put on his head. *George* would not suit the line, and Goldsmith uses *Luke*.

Damiens' bed of steel: in 1757 Damiens, a madman, tried to assassinate Louis XV. of France, and was put to death with frightful tortures. According to Tom Davies (Forster's *Goldsmith*, I. 370, 371) Goldsmith said he meant the rack by "bed of steel," but contemporary accounts relate that Damiens was chained to a bed of iron, on which he was subjected to torture.

THE DESERTED VILLAGE.

DEDICATION.

Sir Joshua Reynolds: the great portrait painter, 1723—1792, a close friend of Goldsmith, Johnson, and Burke. In *Retaliation*, 137 sqq., Goldsmith says:

> "Here Reynolds is laid, and, to tell you my mind,
> He has not left a better or wiser behind:
> His pencil was striking, resistless, and grand;
> His manners were gentle, complying, and bland;
> Still born to improve us in every part,
> His pencil our faces, his manners our heart."

9. **the only dedication:** see p. 41.

16. **depopulation:** see Introduction, p. xiv.

21. **my country excursions:** see Introduction, p. xiv.

27. **indifferent:** middling, mediocre, poor, inferior.

1—34. The poet apostrophizes Auburn as the loveliest of villages, with its genial climate, its happy peasants, its simple sports.

1. **Auburn:** attempts have been made to identify the village. But we must not test a poet's imagination for geographical exactness. No doubt the name was chosen for its sweet sound. The description of the village is partly from Irish sources, partly from English. Irish references occur in lines 5—34, 83—96, 115, 137—250, while England is mentioned in line 57, and seems suggested in line 124, and in Dedication, line 21. See Introduction, p. xiv.

2. **swain:** see *The Traveller*, note to line 48.

3. **smiling:** see *The Traveller*, note to line 122.

4. **parting:** departing. Compare Gray, *Elegy*, 1,
   > "The curfew tolls the knell of parting day."

5. **bowers:** dwelling-places; favourite poetic word for an ideal abode.

6. **seats** : abode, home, where my youth was spent.

9. **paused on** : dwelt on, regarded with fondness.

10—13. See note to line 360 of *The Traveller*.

12. **decent**: comely, handsome. Compare Milton, *Paradise Lost*, III. 644,

> "Before his decent steps a silver wand."

14. **talking age**: old people: abstract for concrete. Compare line 222.

15. **the coming day**: in anticipation he blessed the coming holiday.

16. **remitting** : slackening, ceasing : used intransitively.

17. **village train** : villagers. Goldsmith has various uses of this word. Sometimes it means retinue, as in line 402 of *The Traveller*,

> "Lead stern depopulation in her train."

Sometimes it means band, company, as in line 409 of *The Traveller*,

> "Forced from their homes, a melancholy train."

In fact, Goldsmith uses *train* or *band* with the same meaning, as suits his rhyme : see *The Deserted Village*, 401,

> "Downward they move, a melancholy band."

Again, as in this passage, *village train*, the word is really not much more than an inflection. Compare lines 63, 81, 135, 149, 252, 320, 337.

25. **simply** : artlessly.

27. **mistrustless** : without suspicion.

smutted : blackened, especially with soot. There is a reference to a practical joke in which the victim unconsciously blackens his face to the amusement of the spectators. Compare Addison, *The Spectator*, No. 269, where Sir Roger is speaking about Christmas: "I have always a piece of cold beef and a mince-pie upon the table, and am wonderfully pleased to see my tenants pass away a whole evening in playing their innocent tricks, and smutting one another."

34. **were...are**: past and present in sharp antithesis. The past is emphatic here ; "were but are no longer." Compare Tennyson, *The Princess*, II. 237,

> "You were that Psyche, but what are you now?"

35—50. How different is the scene now ! The village is a shapeless ruin, the haunt of lapwing and bittern. The villagers are exiles in a distant land.

35. lawn : see note to line 319 of *The Traveller*.

37. See 275 sqq. and notes.

40. No longer fully cultivated, the fields have lost their former show of crops. Compare line 280.

44. **bittern** : a bird allied to the heron, solitary, inhabiting reedy and marshy places, noted for its peculiar bellowing or booming cry. When assailed, it fights fiercely with claws and bill. Goldsmith, *Animated Nature*, III. 242, ed. 1818, says its cry "is like the interrupted bellowing of a bull, but hollower and louder, and is heard at a mile's distance as if issuing from some formidable being that resided at the bottom of the waters." Hence the bittern is called Bull of the Bog: as Scott, *Guy Mannering*, ch. i. It is also called Miredrum: compare Scott, *Lady of the Lake*, I. st. 31,

> "And the bittern sound his drum,
>
> Booming from the sedgy shallow."

The Bible makes this bird a sign of desolation : Isaiah xiv. 23, xxxiv. 11, Zephaniah ii. 14.

50. Note the effect of the repetition of *far*.

51—56. Woe to the land where wealth increases and population decreases ! Nothing can make up for a lost peasantry.

51. **ill...ills** : Goldsmith has been censured for the jingle. When, as here, the words are different parts of speech, or when, as *seats* in lines 6 and 13, they differ in meaning, such repetition of similar sounds had better, for the sake of clearness, be avoided in serious writing Compare Scott, *Lord of the Isles*, I. st. 27,

> "When Comyn fell beneath the knife
>
> Of that fell homicide The Bruce";

where the words differ in meaning and in kind.

There is no objection to the repetition of *breath* in line 54.

53 sq. Compare Burns, *Cotter's Saturday Night*, 165,

> "Princes and lords are but the breath of kings";

and "A Man's a Man," 25 sq.,

> "A prince can mak a belted knight,
>
> A marquis, duke, and a' that."

57—62. Long ago, in happier times, England was a land of peasants, hard-working, healthy and contented.

58. **rood** : a quarter of an acre. It is of course a poetic exaggeration to say that every acre supported four men. This cry of the decay

of peasants had been loudly uttered before, in the xvith century, when many small holdings were turned into large sheep farms : see Sir Thomas More's *Utopia*, and Latimer's *Sermons*. The word *rood* originally meant the measuring-stick or pole. In fact *rood* and *rod* are double forms from Anglo-Saxon *ród*, a cross, properly a pole. *Rood*, cross, occurs in *Holyrood*, *rood-screen*, etc.

62. Note the epigrammatic touch in this line. He was truly rich because he had no riches. Compare what is said of the Swiss : *The Traveller*, 175 sqq.

63—74. But now those who have grown wealthy by trading have driven out the peasants and destroyed the villages. The simple happy life is now gone.

63. train: see note to line 17.

65 sqq.: see 275 sqq. and notes.

74. manners: see note to line 228 of *The Traveller*.

75—82. This fate has overtaken Auburn, and the poet is pained at the difference.

76. glades : open grassy spots ; what he also calls lawns.
forlorn : deserted.
tyrant's power : the proprietor who evicted the inhabitants.

79. It was only in imagination that Goldsmith returned to Lissoy. The sober truth is expressed in the next passage. In spite of his hopes (85 sqq.), he never went back to Ireland (98). See Introduction, p. x.
many a year elapsed: nominative absolute. So in 157 and 393.

83—96. In all his many wanderings, he hoped to return to Auburn, and there end his days in peace.

87. husband : use with economy.
taper : light is a frequent metaphor for life.

89 sqq. In a letter of 1758 Goldsmith looks forward to the time when he shall sit by Kilmore fireside and " recount the various adventures of a hard-fought life, laugh over the follies of the day, join his flute to the harpsichord and forget that he ever starved in those streets."

93. an hare : see note to line 34 of *The Traveller*.
hounds and horns pursue : the figure of zeugma. *Pursue* goes properly only with *hounds*.

97—112. But such retirement can never be the poet's. Happy is the man who after a life of toil lives in retirement and glides imperceptibly from earth to heaven.

99. **crowns**: finishes, perfects, rounds off. Goldsmith uses *crown* to mean also load, heap, reward: see lines 85, 351; and *The Traveller*, 11, 17, 45.

104. **explore**: ransack the mine and bring up its treasures.

105. **porter**: door-keeper: a different word from *porter*, a carrier of burdens.

guilty state: his gorgeous dress bought with ill-gotten gains.

106. **spurn**: a strong expression for contemptuous driving away · it means literally to kick.

famine: the famished, the destitute: abstract for concrete.

107. **latter end**: a euphemism for death.

110. Sir Joshua Reynolds painted a picture of "An Old Man," afterwards engraved as "Resignation," with the inscription: "This attempt to express a character in *The Deserted Village* is dedicated to Dr Goldsmith, by his sincere friend and admirer, Joshua Reynolds."

112. **be past**: subjunctive mood in a temporal clause referring to the future, formerly a common usage. Compare Scott, *Marmion*, IV. st. 32,

> "There stays the minstrel till he fling
> His hand o'er every Border string,
> And fit his harp the pomp to sing."

113—136. How sweet it was in the evening to hear the mingled sounds of the happy village! But now, save one old woman, there is not one inhabitant left. Note the beauty of these lines.

113. **sweet was the sound**: see note to line 203 of *The Traveller*.
yonder: see note to line 103 of *The Traveller*.

115. **careless**: as I sauntered along, my mind free from care.

117 sqq. Each line represents a scene like a picture.

117. **responsive**: the swain and the milkmaid sang alternate verses. Compare Gray, *Ode on the Spring*, 5 sq.,

> "The Attic warbler pours her throat,
> Responsive to the cuckoo's note."

milkmaid: Goldsmith had pleasant recollections of a milkmaid's singing. In *The Bee*, No. 2, he says: "The music of Mattei is dissonance to what I felt when our old dairymaid sang me into tears with Johnny Armstrong's Last Good Night, or the cruelty of Barbara Allen.'

sung : the past indicative of *sing* and similar verbs had formerly two forms, but good usage now sanctions only *sang, rang,* etc. The *u* form is restricted in prose to the participle, though used in poetry also for the indicative.

118. **sober :** walking sedately, staid, not skipping or frisking. Compare Gray, *Elegy,* 2,

"The lowing herd wind slowly o'er the lea."

119. Contrast this line with 118, both in sound and in scene.

120. Scott, *Old Mortality,* ch. i., describes, at greater length, the rush from school on a summer evening.

122. **spoke :** showed, disclosed. Compare Scott, *Marmion,* I. st. 5,

"Yet lines of thought upon his cheek
Did deep design and counsel speak."

vacant : this line is frequently quoted and misapplied as if *vacant* meant empty, silly. But here, and in line 257, it means free from anxiety, unconcerned, light-hearted. Compare *careless* in line 115; and *The Vicar,* ch. v., " Every morning waked us to a repetition of toil ; but the evening repaid it with vacant hilarity."

124. **pause :** the interval between bursts of song. It is by poetic licence that Goldsmith places the nightingale in Ireland.

126. **fluctuate :** move like waves of the sea, rise and fall. See Introduction, p. xvi.

gale : breeze. See note to line 47 of *The Traveller.*

128. **bloomy flush :** those in the full bloom, the freshness and vigour, of life have disappeared.

130. **plashy :** full of puddles, muddy pools.

132. **mantling :** spreading like a mantle. Compare Milton, *Paradise Lost,* IV. 258 sq.,

" O'er which the mantling vine
Lays forth her purple grape."

For another use, see line 248.

134. **nightly :** see note to line 198 of *The Traveller.*

136. **historian :** here simply one who tells the story. Obsolete in this sense, says *The New English Dictionary.*

137—162. There by the copse stood the house of the village preacher, well beloved and holy, a man of integrity and benevolence.

140. Some consider the village preacher to be a picture of Goldsmith's father, others of his brother Henry. Probably the picture

contains traits from both these and also from his uncle Contarine.
Goldsmith pictures two other clergymen, Dr Primrose in *The Vicar*,
and the father of the Man in Black, *Citizen of the World*, Letter XXVII.
Compare Chaucer's Parish Priest, *The Prologue*, 477 sqq.; Dryden,
The Character of a Good Parson; and Cowper's Good Preacher, *The
Task*, II. 337 sqq.

mansion: house, as in 195, and 238. The word is now regularly
used of a large stately residence. See note to line 167 of *The Traveller*.

142. **forty pounds**: was the Rev. Henry Goldsmith's income: see
Dedication to *The Traveller*, line 11. This amount, or less, was
common in the XVIIIth century. Goldsmith makes Dr Primrose have
thirty-five pounds from his first benefice, fifteen from his second: *The
Vicar*, ch. ii. and iii.

143. Goldsmith, like Johnson and Cowper, seems to have held
that a good life could be more easily lived in the country than in the
town. See Johnson, *London*, 5 sq., and Cowper, *The Task*, I. 749 sqq.

ran his godly race: life is frequently called a race, as in Hebrews
xii. 1, "Let us run with patience the race that is set before us."

race is cognate object of *run*, that is, an object of kindred meaning
to the verb. It is often kindred in origin as well as meaning, as
Shakespeare, *The Tempest*, I. 1. 70,

"I would fain die a dry death."

144. **place**: the benefice he held.

145. He was no time-server, did not change his opinions to win
preferment.

148. **raise...rise**: contrasted both in meaning and in sound.

149. **vagrant train**: vagrants. See note to line 17.

151. **long-remembered**: the remembrance of his visits extended
over many years.

152. **aged**: transferred epithet.

155. **broken soldier**: explained by some as disbanded, the peace
of 1763 having flooded the country with disbanded soldiers: see
Lecky's *History of England in the XVIIIth Century*, III. 135. In
The Vicar, ch. iii., we hear of "an old broken soldier that was to be
whipped through the town for dog-stealing." Others take the word
as disabled, and refer to the lines which follow. Compare Campbell,
The Soldier's Dream, 22,

"And fain was their war-broken soldier to stay."

bade: past indicative form incorrectly used instead of the regular participle *bidden*. See note to line 358 of *The Traveller*.

156. **talked the night away**: compare Scott, *Lord of the Isles*, II. st. 10,

> " Brother, it better suits the time
> To chase the night with Ferrand's rhyme."

157. **tales of sorrow done**: after he had finished his grim stories.

159. **glow**: burn with emotion.

161. **careless**: regardless, unconcerned: agrees with *him* suggested by *his* in next line.

162. **pity…charity**: note the antithesis. *Pity* is the feeling roused by the sight of woe and need, which seeks to relieve without enquiry: *charity* is restrained by prudence and asks if the help is deserved. In *The Citizen of the World*, Letters XXVI., XXVII., the Man in Black preaches "charity" and practises "pity."

163—170. He was diligent in his duty: by example as well as by precept he taught his flock how to live.

164. Better that his failings should be such an excess of benevolence than that too much prudence and economy should make him a miser.

171—176. No one could give more consolation to the dying, whether racked by pain or terrified by guilt.

171. **parting life**: used figuratively for a dying man, called *the struggling soul* and *the trembling wretch*, as Goldsmith brings forward different aspects of the death bed. For *parting*=dying, compare Gray, *Elegy*, 89,

> "On some fond breast the parting soul relies."

172. **dismayed**: deprived the dying man of strength of body and mind.

177—192. In church, his unaffected piety made the truth doubly powerful. After service, the whole congregation, children and all, crowded round him to show their love.

181 sqq. Note the graphic description of the scene.

189 sqq. A beautiful simile. Compare 167 sq.

193—216. Yonder by the fence stood the village school. The master was stern and severe, yet kind hearted. The villagers thought him profoundly learned, especially when he argued with the parson.

194. **unprofitably**: Goldsmith seems here to regard nature in a utilitarian spirit, as if he should ask why the useless furze should be covered with golden blossoms.

198. Thomas Byrne of Lissoy was the original of the village schoolmaster. See Introduction, p. ix.

199. **boding**: foreboding, anticipating ill.

206. **fault**: sounds to us a bad rhyme with *aught*, but Goldsmith did not pronounce the *l*. In *Edwin and Angelina* he rhymes *fault* with *sought*. Pope rhymes it with *ought, thought, taught*; Swift with *wrought*; Dryden with *thought*. Dr Johnson says in his *Dictionary*, "The *l* is sometimes sounded, and sometimes mute. In conversation it is generally suppressed." When introduced into Middle English, the word was written and pronounced *faute*. In the xvith century *l* unpronounced was inserted to show the etymology: the word is ultimately from Latin *fallere*. Finally the pronunciation conformed to the spelling. Similarly *c* was inserted in *verdict* and has influenced the pronunciation; but the intrusion of *c* in *victuals* and *b* in *doubt* has left the pronunciation unchanged.

207 sqq. Note the irony. While praising the master from the standpoint of the villagers, Goldsmith hints that his learning was not profound.

208. **cipher**: work the elementary rules of arithmetic. The word *cipher* meant originally o, being derived through Old French from an Arabian word = zero or nought: then it was applied to all the Arabic numerals. It has other meanings, as secret writing, and monogram.

209. **terms and tides presage**: act like a calendar to let them know the fixed terms and the festivals. Some explain *terms* as those of the law courts—Hilary, Easter, Trinity, Michaelmas; but the word may mean rent or quarter days—Ladyday, Midsummer, Michaelmas, Christmas. For *tide*, compare *Eastertide, Whitsuntide, Christmastide*.

210. **gauge**: measure the capacity of barrels, etc.

213. They had length and sound, if not sense. Such words were used by the Squire to vanquish Moses in *The Vicar*, ch. vii., "The premises being thus settled, I proceed to observe that the concatenation of self-existences, proceeding in a reciprocal duplicate ratio, naturally produce a problematical dialogism, which in some measure proves that the essence of spirituality may be referred to the second

predicable.......Whether do you judge the analytical investigation of the first part of my Enthymeme deficient secundum quoad or quoad minus."

learned: the adjective is dissyllabic, while the participle, as in line 199, is monosyllabic.

217—236. Close to yonder thorn stood the village inn, a centre for news and merriment.

Compare the inn scene in Burns, *Tam o' Shanter*, and in Cowper, *The Task*, IV. 466 sqq.

222. **grey-beard mirth**: old merry-makers, merry old men. Note the double figure of speech: by metonymy *grey-beard* stands for *old*; and the abstract *mirth* is put for the concrete *merry-makers*.

toil: workers, labourers: abstract for concrete.

223. Note the genial irony.

227. **nicely**: carefully, neatly.

228. **clock that clicked**: example of onomatopoeia, where the sound echoes the sense. Compare *The Traveller*, 412; and Tennyson, *The Princess*, VII. 206 sq.,

> "The moan of doves in immemorial elms,
> And murmuring of innumerable bees."

229 sqq. Compare Goldsmith, *Description of an author's bed-chamber*, 10 sqq.:

> "The humid wall with paltry pictures spread:
> The royal game of goose was there in view,
> And the twelve rules the royal martyr drew;
>
> *   *   *   *   *
>
> And five cracked teacups dressed the chimney board;
> A nightcap decked his brows instead of bay,
> A cap by night—a stocking all the day!"

232. **the twelve good rules**: were printed beneath a woodcut of King Charles's Execution, and frequently hung framed on the wall of a room. The rules, reputed to have been found in the king's study, are: 1. Urge no healths. 2. Profane no divine ordinances. 3. Touch no state matters. 4. Reveal no secrets. 5. Pick no quarrels. 6. Make no comparisons. 7. Maintain no ill opinions. 8. Keep no bad company. 9. Encourage no vice. 10. Make no long meals. 11. Repeat no grievances. 12. Lay no wagers.

the royal game of goose: is described by Strutt, *Sports and*

Pastimes, IV. ch. 2. The game consists in moving—according to the throws of dice—through sixty-two compartments marked on a card, to reach a central open space. At every fourth and fifth compartment in succession a goose is depicted. Why it is called royal, is not clear.

236. **chimney**: fire-place.

237—250. The inn is gone. Gone too are the guests and the landlord.

240. Because he gives orders as a master and is served by others.

241 sqq. Note the repetition of *no more* at the beginning of each member of the sentence: the figure called anaphora. Compare 310 sqq., and *The Traveller*, 397 sqq.

242. Compare Cowper (as cited in note to line 217),

"The craftsman there
Takes a Lethean leave of all his toil;
Smith, cobbler, joiner, he that plies the shears,
And he that kneads the dough; all loud alike,
All learned and all drunk."

244. **woodman's ballad**: seems to refer to a Robin Hood ballad, or some other of the greenwood songs. *Woodman* means here hunter, sportsman: the older meaning, as in Shakespeare and Milton, and the only one in Dr Johnson's *Dictionary*.

245 sq. A graphic picture of absorbed attention.

248. **mantling bliss**: the gladdening ale is called *bliss* by the figure of metonymy, effect for cause. See Introduction, p. xvi.

mantling: foaming, frothing. See note to line 132.

251—264. These simple joys, however much despised by the great, are dear to the poet, and far excel the laborious pleasures of the fashionable world.

252. **lowly train**: see note to line 17.

256. **first-born sway**: the predominance that belongs by right to the first-born.

257. **vacant**: see note to line 122.

258. Compare Milton, *Paradise Lost*, II. 185,

"Unrespited, unpitied, unreprieved";
and Scott, *Lay of the Last Minstrel*, VI. st. 1,

"Unwept, unhonoured, and unsung."

259. **long pomp**: compare 317: a long procession, gilded coaches with outriders and footmen.

masquerade: compare 319. An entertainment where masks and other disguises were worn, and dancing, etc. engaged in: very popular in the XVIIIth century. At a masquerade in 1785 there were represented such characters as a travelling fiddler, a native of Otaheite, a bellman, a Turk, a Mercury, Night, a Laplander, harlequins, orange girls, milk girls, haymakers, sailors, witches, etc. A masquerade is described in Fanny Burney's *Cecilia*, II. ch. 3. See also *Social England*, v. 186 sqq.

260. **freaks of wanton wealth**: whims of capricious rich people.

264. **be**: subjunctive mood in indirect question: a usage formerly common.

265—286. A splendid land is not necessarily happy. If useful products decrease while wealth increases, then the splendour is but a sham.

270. **Folly**: personified represents the thoughtless inhabitants of the country who rejoice at the influx of wealth.

274. In other words it does not "make two ears of corn, or two blades of grass, to grow upon a spot of ground where only one grew before": Swift, *Gulliver's Travels*, Part II. ch. 7.

275 sqq. See lines 35 and 65. It is generally held that Goldsmith was especially thinking of evictions carried out at Lissoy by General Napier, who had purchased land in the neighbourhood. Wishing to enlarge the park, he had to get several families removed from their homes.

279. **silken**: transferred epithet: the robe of silk in which he lazily reclines.

282. **spurns**: see note to line 106.

283 sq. Home products which should have been kept in the country are exported to all parts of the world in exchange for every kind of superfluous luxury.

287—302. When a beauty loses her natural charms, she seeks artificial aids, but in vain. So the land that is ruined by luxury, may appear splendid; but when its peasants are driven away by famine, it is in reality a grave.

287. **fair female**: would not be now used in this context. As synonymous with *woman*, *female* is now usually avoided by good writers unless contempt is expressed.

plain: simple, without embellishment. Note that *plain* applied to features is often a euphemism for homely, ugly.

294. **glaring**: transferred epithet from *dress*. It is here, as often, used of excessively bright colours, showy.

297. **verging**: agrees with *it* suggested by *its*.

302. **a garden and a grave**: epigrammatic antithesis.

303—308. Where can the evicted peasant go? Even the commons are seized by the rich.

305 sqq. Much of the common land, that is, land in which the inhabitants of a village had common rights of pasturages, etc., was being enclosed at this time and turned into farms. The increasing population demanded increase of agricultural produce. Between 1760 and 1770 about a thousand Enclosure Bills were passed by Parliament; and in George III.'s reign over six million acres were enclosed. See *Social England*, vol. v., pp. 617, 623, etc.; and Bright's *History of England*, vol. III., p. 1150.

307. **sons of wealth**: rich men. See 313, *sons of pleasure*, lovers of pleasure. This is a common usage in Hebrew, and appears frequently in the Bible, as "the son of perdition," John xvii. 12; "children of the light," Luke xvi. 8.

309—336. If he goes to the city, he sees the grim contrast between the toiler and the gay courtier, between the pomps of the proud and the gibbet of dishonour, between the heartless lover of pleasure and the homeless outcast.

311. **baneful**: life-destroying, pernicious. *Bane*, harm, destruction, is from Anglo-Saxon *bana*, murderer.

315. **brocade**: here means a fabric woven with a pattern of raised figures in gold and silver. In these days the courtiers really "glittered." At the King's birthday ball in 1781, the Prince of Wales wore a bright-coloured pink silk coat, richly embroidered with silver, and a waistcoat of silver tissue.

316. **artist**: artisan. Goldsmith also uses *artist* of a cobbler.

318. **gibbet**: as capital punishment was the penalty for many minor offences in the XVIIIth century (see Histories; *The Vicar*, ch. xxvii.; Dickens, *Barnaby Rudge*, chs. xxxvii., lxv.), and as all executions were in public, the gibbet was a familiar sight, an upright post with a projecting arm, from which the dead body dangled in chains for long after the execution. Compare a remark by Horace Walpole,

circa 1760: "It is shocking to think what a shambles the country has grown. Seventeen were executed this morning."

319. **dome** : house.

322. The grand coaches of the wealthy, richly gilded and brightly painted, accompanied by troops of servants carrying torches.

323. In the previous instances *here* is followed by *there*, but for emphasis in the final contrast, someone is supposed to intervene with the remark : "Surely no sorrow mars this joyous scene."

330. See Introduction, p. xvi.

336. **wheel**: spinning-wheel. In those days every country girl learned to spin.

country brown : russet homespun. Dr Johnson in his *Dictionary* says: "In some places, the rustics still dye cloths spun at home with bark, which must make them *russet*."

337—340. Can it be that the inhabitants of Auburn are among the hungry and the wretched ?

341—352. No. They are far away from cool, green Auburn, away in the wilds of America, under burning suns, in horrid woods, beset by deadly animals and reptiles, by murderous Indians, and by fierce tornadoes.

342. **convex world**: the part of the globe rising in convex form between Europe and America. This term of mathematical geography is somewhat out of place.

344. **Altama** : the river Altamaha, in Georgia, U.S.A.

murmurs to: in sympathy with. The idea of Nature showing sympathy with man, or antipathy to him, has been called the pathetic fallacy. A striking example occurs in Shakespeare, *King Lear*, III. 2. 21 sqq.

345 sqq. Compare *The Traveller*, 413 sqq.

349. Goldsmith, *Animated Nature*, III. 202, speaks of America as a region "where the birds excel rather in the beauty of their plumage than the sweetness of their notes."

Compare Thomson, *Summer*, 738 sqq.,

> "But if she (Nature) bids them shine,
> Arrayed in all the beauteous beams of day,
> Yet frugal still, she humbles them in song."

350. Compare *Animated Nature*, II. 332, where of one kind of bat it is said: "In the morning, at peep of day, they are seen sticking

upon the tops of the trees, and clinging to each other, like bees when they swarm, or like large clusters of cocoa."

351. **rank** : vigorous in growth, rich.

352. **death** : poison : by metonymy the effect is put for the cause. The scorpion, he means, eats poisonous plants to supply its venom.

355. **tigers** : pumas. In *Animated Nature*, II. 170, Goldsmith says that the animal called by some the couguar (=puma), and by others the red tiger, he ranks along with the tiger of the East, because the two closely resemble each other.

360. **grassy-vested** : see note to line 108 of *The Traveller*.

362. **thefts of harmless love** : stolen kisses.

363—384. How sad was their last day in Auburn. Old and young, strong and weak, they had to go, but could scarcely tear themselves away.

365. **exiles** : called so by anticipation : the figure of prolepsis.

368. **seats** : dwellings, homes : so in line 6.

370. Note the repeated words in this line : a favourite poetical device. Compare Shelley, *To a Skylark*,

"And singing still dost soar, and soaring ever singest."

380. **cot** : cottage.

381. **thoughtless** : too young to understand.

384. **silent** : transferred epithet to *manliness*, as his silence is the result and the sign of manliness.

385—394. And what have we got in exchange for these? Luxury, which gives a false appearance of prosperity to a country and then ruins it.

389 sqq. See note to *The Traveller*, 144.

392. A swollen mass of misery, gross and unwieldy.

395 *to end*. The ruin is already begun. In imagination, the poet sees the best and most virtuous peasants moving down to the ship that will carry them over the sea. With them goes the spirit of poesy. That spirit he invokes to teach erring man to despise the mad pursuit of wealth, and to learn that a land may be poor and yet happy.

397 sqq. The intensity of the poet's emotion justifies this use of the figure of vision, by which the absent is vividly described as present. Compare the passage in Byron, *Childe Harold*, IV. st. 140, beginning :

"I see before me the Gladiator lie."

398. **virtues**: enumerated in lines 403 sqq. They are the abstract representations of the emigrants mentioned in lines 371 sqq.

399. **anchoring**: lying at anchor.

402. **shore...strand**: are evidently distinguished in meaning. *Strand* here means that part nearest the sea, the beach of sand, shingle, etc., on which the waves break, while *shore* is the margin of the land.

409. Except for what Goldsmith was himself doing,

" To catch the heart, or strike for honest fame,"

English poetry had at this time sunk very low.

411. **nymph**: was in the XVIIIth century a favourite poetical synonym for *maid*.

412 sqq. We must not take seriously what is said of poetry as causing Goldsmith "shame" and "woe." It brought him fame and happiness; and his poverty was not the fault of poetry. Compare another remark of Goldsmith's in a similar strain : "Whenever I write anything, the public make a point to know nothing about it."

417 sqq. Gray, *Progress of Poesy*, 54 sqq., speaks of poetry cheering the dreary polar regions and finding a home in the tropics.

418. **Torno's cliffs**: Torneå is the name of a lake and a river in the north of Sweden. Pronounce *å* as *o*.

Pambamarca's side: a mountain mentioned by Goldsmith as near Quito, in Peru : *Animated Nature*, I. 220.

419. **equinoctial fervours**: equatorial heat. The equator is called the equinoctial line.

428. **laboured mole**: mound or breakwater reared with much labour.

427—430. Attributed to Dr Johnson.

430. **sky**: used figuratively for storms.

INDEX TO THE NOTES.

The references are to the pages.

For EU product safety concerns, contact us at Calle de José Abascal, 56–1°, 28003 Madrid, Spain or eugpsr@cambridge.org.

www.ingramcontent.com/pod-product-compliance
Ingram Content Group UK Ltd.
Pitfield, Milton Keynes, MK11 3LW, UK
UKHW020312140625
459647UK00018B/1838